Maria
I once was lost!

Sanity 365

Norm

Sanity 365

Daily Help For Sane Living

Norm Sharkey

BALBOA
PRESS
A DIVISION OF HAY HOUSE

Copyright © 2005, 2011 Norm Sharkey

All rights reserved. No part of this book may be used or reproduced by any means, graphic, electronic, or mechanical, including photocopying, recording, taping or by any information storage retrieval system without the written permission of the publisher except in the case of brief quotations embodied in critical articles and reviews.

Balboa Press books may be ordered through booksellers or by contacting:

*Balboa Press
A Division of Hay House
1663 Liberty Drive
Bloomington, IN 47403
www.balboapress.com
1-(877) 407-4847*

Because of the dynamic nature of the Internet, any web addresses or links contained in this book may have changed since publication and may no longer be valid. The views expressed in this work are solely those of the author and do not necessarily reflect the views of the publisher, and the publisher hereby disclaims any responsibility for them.

The author of this book does not dispense medical advice or prescribe the use of any technique as a form of treatment for physical, emotional, or medical problems without the advice of a physician, either directly or indirectly. The intent of the author is only to offer information of a general nature to help you in your quest for emotional and spiritual well-being. In the event you use any of the information in this book for yourself, which is your constitutional right, the author and the publisher assume no responsibility for your actions.

*Any people depicted in stock imagery provided by Thinkstock are models, and such images are being used for illustrative purposes only.
Certain stock imagery © Thinkstock.*

*ISBN: 978-1-4525-3743-6 (e)
ISBN: 978-1-4525-3740-5 (sc)
ISBN: 978-1-4525-3742-9 (hc)*

Library of Congress Control Number: 2011914334

Printed in the United States of America

Balboa Press rev. date: 8/11/2011

The Our House Reality

I have arrived here because I can no longer escape from myself! I have finally come to understand that I am the problem, not others! My secrets keep me sick and hopeless! Through being open and honest with other addicts, I can stop being the angel of my dreams and the devil of my fears. I can become real and free. This is my reality.

Our House
Recovery Values

1. We admitted we were powerless over any kind of drugs and our life had become a mess.

2. Through being open and honest with fellow addicts, we came to know a power we could depend on, called God.

3. With the help of God and our friends, we took an honest look at ourselves and became willing to change the things that were keeping us high.

4. Since we had harmed many people, we attempted to make things right with them.

5. We continued to take a look at ourselves on a daily basis, and when anything bothered us, we talked about it.

6. With God and our friends, we tried to give other addicts what we had received and to follow these values in our daily living.

Acknowledgments

Anyone who has touched my life in any way deserves credit for Sanity 365, including especially my biological family, my family through marriage, my addiction family, and God as I understand God. I do not want to embarrass anyone by mentioning them by name, or hurt anyone by not mentioning them by name. Anyone who knows me should be mentioned, but I am positive that there would not be enough room for all the names. You know who you are, so thank you. Since the late '70s I have had an idea for a book of this sort, so you can see that I am a procrastinator. Many people have passed on to the hereafter since then, but they too should receive credit because they to are often in my thoughts. Thank you, one and all.

—Norm

**To Joey,
my daughter, whom I love dearly**

Introduction

Many, many methods had been developed over the years to help addicts in the process of getting clean and staying clean. If you are a person who has had his or her life kidnapped by drugs and have found freedom using some of these methods, I say thank you for letting me join you. It matters not what methods we use to stay drug free; the important thing is that we do. Each of us who has survived the Insanity is one less problem for society and one more person with an answer for the people who are still kidnapped. Drugs don't just kidnap the user; they take the whole family hostage. Drugs have become a plague in our society and world wide. Families stand by helplessly as their loved ones are devoured by this culture. The money spent on drugs by one addict, in one day, could probably feed a whole family in some countries for a month or longer. The wasted money is just a small part of the devastation caused by drugs. The chaos those drugs create within in a family has no limits, even to the point of murder, physically and mentally! Any of us who have escaped should understand what the word gratitude means. I have been blessed with a drug free life for several years now, and I am also surrounded by many, many exceptional people who have helped me stay this way.

Saying thank you to all these people does not even begin to express the gratitude I have for them, so I hope the daily reminders that I put to paper will some how get that message across. To those of you whom I have not met yet, some of these daily reminders may make no sense at all. For that I apologize. My only purpose for Sanity 365 is that in some way it may give you an extra little lift at some point during your day, reminding you that the war is over and you survived it! We all know people who are still fighting. Don't forget them! To the family of the user, I also understand the helplessness that you feel, since I am sure that you have tried everything that has been suggested in the way of solutions. If, so far, the results have been negative, don't give up hope! Don't give the kidnapped one the excuse that you don't care. Make the addict accept the responsibility for his or her own situation. You are not forcing drugs on them. Seek help for yourself, because your own sanity will continue to be tested.

—Norm

January

**Daily Reminder
January 1**

Think about it!

A new year and a new life have begun. For a change, we can look ahead with hope. When someone says "Happy New Year" to us, we can, for once, believe it can be. On past New Year's Days, we were either still stoned, coming down, or starting to get stoned again. We felt that drugs were the only way to be happy. Nothing changed, except things got worse! Happy Clean can change that!

HOPE

Trying is good! Doing is better!

Today, I want to live a better life. I must change my thinking from loser to winner. I know I am not hopeless. I can change, and I will change.

Daily Reminder
January 2

Think about it!

In our daily lives, we became little more than robots. We got up, got stoned, and planned how we would get more drugs, who we would use for our pleasure, and who we would rip off or do in. Always me, me, me! The animal inside us called addiction needed to be fed. We were not able to choose what we would do; we had to obey the animal. Today, we can choose!

SLAVE

Trying is good! Doing is better!

With help from people, I can choose to stay clean today. I want to believe that God will also help me, if I ask.

Daily Reminder
January 3

Think about it!

When it may seem like a bad life, it's a good life. When we are clean and we have problems, we can still work them out in time. When we deal with the problems or someone helps us with them, we become stronger. **REALITY** The strength we get from this process allows us to deal with future problems. So what may look like a bad life situation is still a good life. Drugs never made our lives better, always worse.

Trying is good! Doing is better!

There is no quick cure. We took a long time to mess up our lives; we need time to clean things up. The Six Values will help us clean things up day by day.

Norm Sharkey

Daily Reminder
January 4

Think about it!

Until we got help, drugs were the "Higher Power" in our lives! We needed drugs to help plan our day. We did nothing until we stuck a needle in our arm, snorted coke, popped pills, or smoked a joint. We found nothing odd about that. For us, this was normal. If we are to stay clean, we must find a new power. Can I rely only on people for my help?

STRENGTH

Trying is good! Doing is better!

Today, I will try to connect with that "New Power." I will talk to other addicts to see how they did this, and then I will try myself.

Daily Reminder
January 5

Think about it!

If you are a normal addict, you will be upset if your life doesn't turn around right away. We are used to instant results from our years of using. If one pill didn't work, a handful did. The clean life is different. Sometimes the answer may come right away, but most of our answers take time. I must be willing to let time sort out my problems.

PATIENCE

Trying is good! Doing is better!

God helps those who wait, as long as they work like hell while they wait. Pray for potatoes, but grab a hoe!

Daily Reminder
January 6

Think about it!

There is no easy, fast way to get better. If there were, we would have found it by now. We would be known as experts, but we are not experts. We have simply found a way to live without drugs, and to be happy most of the time. We may not be happy all the time, just as we were not happy all the time on drugs.

SLOW DOWN

Trying is good! Doing is better!

When we feel down, if we talk to someone else, we may see that our problems are not as bad as we thought. Who can I help today?

Daily Reminder
January 7

Think about it!

As users, we became more and more selfish! We thought only about ourselves and what would make us happy. Anyone who got in our way was removed. Anything that got in our way was also removed.

ME! ME! ME!

We let nothing stop us in our search for happiness. Are we prepared to do the same to stay clean and happy? What must we do?

Trying is good! Doing is better!

Each day we must be ready to listen to people who have some answers. If we know it all, why are we here? If staying clean is your problem, we can help.

Norm Sharkey

**Daily Reminder
January 8**

Think about it!

We have learned, we hope, that the happiness we got from drugs came with a big price tag. We sold our souls, our bodies, and other people's things, and at the end, we were far from happy. Each day when we came to and thought of what we had done the day before, we had to get stoned again! On and on it went! Is there a better way?

THE COST

Trying is good! Doing is better!

How do I find a better way to be happy? Will someone please help me to find the "happiness train"?

Daily Reminder
January 9

Think about it!

When we finally come down and begin to feel somewhat healthy, that in itself is enough to make us happy. As the days go on, we see some things we have to change if we are to stay happy. If we don't stay happy when we are clean, we will turn back to drugs. What can I do today to stay happy?

CHANGE

Trying is good! Doing is better!

Each day we must be ready to look at and change what was keeping us high. Am I ready to do that today?

Norm Sharkey

Daily Reminder
January 10

Think about it!

There are times when we may want to be alone. That is okay if there is a good reason to be alone. If we are trying to look at our past so we can change and become better people, we may need to be alone for a little while. We have to be honest about our reasons for being alone or we may go backward. Am I going in drive or reverse?

GO ON

Trying is good! Doing is better!

Please help me to be honest with myself and others so I can continue to move forward in drive.

Daily Reminder
January 11

Think about it!

When we came to on any day, we did not have much purpose for living. We did not think we were worth anything to anyone, let alone to ourselves. Success was not a word we used much. We were without hope even though we tried to pretend otherwise. We needed something to give us hope!

HELP

Trying is good! Doing is better!

The six values are another way to look at hope. Many people have felt hopeless and have come to feel worth something again. Have I talked to someone today?

Norm Sharkey

Daily Reminder
January 12

Think about it!

Believing in ourselves seems to be something that happens slowly. Since we are people who look for instant results, we have a hard time dealing with this. The more we talk to new people and try to help them, the more we begin to believe we are useful. When we help others, we help ourselves.

LOVE

Trying is good! Doing is better!

When we discover the only thing that really matters in life is the privilege of helping others, we then discover God. Do I understand this yet?

Daily Reminder
January 13

Think about it!

ACTION

If we are to stay clean happily, we will have to find a belief in some power bigger than ourselves. That doesn't mean you have to get holy right away. It usually happens as you begin to believe in yourself. Helping others, helping yourself, and receiving help from others will lead you to God!

Trying is good! Doing is better!

It doesn't matter to anyone who your Higher Power may be. It could be God or Jesus Christ, Buddha, Allah or the fence post.

Norm Sharkey

Daily Reminder
January 14

Think about it!

Rather than being losers, we have the privilege of becoming winners. Since we have been there and done that, when we talk to addicts about ourselves, they will see we really know what we're talking about. When was the last time anyone really listened to you? Perhaps it was when you were giving them free dope—but only until it was gone. Now you will discover that people do listen. What a good feeling!

USEFUL

Trying is good! Doing is better!

I know if I want to feel worth something, I must help others feel the same way! When do I start?

Daily Reminder
January 15

Think about it!

HANG IN

If you don't stand for something, you'll fall for anything. That's where we were when drugs came into our lives! We didn't believe in anyone or anything. We were sitting ducks for all the promises drugs give. We made good partners because we weren't real and the promises made by drugs weren't real. Do these things make sense now?

Trying is good! Doing is better!

If I want to stay clean, I have to get my hand on the wheel of something that's real! Am I getting there?

Norm Sharkey

Daily Reminder
January 16

Think about it!

I had a hard time accepting drugs were not real. A young child has a hard time accepting Santa Claus is not real. For me, drugs were a good replacement for Santa Claus. When I found out there was no Santa Claus, Christmas was never the same. When drugs found me, I could dream again; however, the dreams became nightmares.

FAKE

Trying is good! Doing is better!

Accepting what is real and what is not real is the beginning of recovery. This is one of the hardest things to do! Have I made some progress?

Daily Reminder
January 17

Think about it!

SELFISH

Me, me, me was all I thought about! Did I look good? Did I feel good? Was I happy? Was I sad? No one else mattered but me. People and things were just to be used for my enjoyment! People were only things to be used. If I hurt them— so what? It was only when I started to get hurt, that my thinking changed. Poor me is hurt.

Trying is good! Doing is better!

People are not things; I'm not a thing. I need to be loved, and people need to be loved! When will I start to love myself and others?

Daily Reminder
January 18

Think about it!

If someone called me a useless, worthless piece of garbage, I would want to kill him or her! However, that is what I called myself when I was using. I needed

WORTH

drugs to make decisions, and most of my decisions involved getting more drugs! I refuse to feel useless and worthless again! I refuse to use drugs again!

Trying is good! Doing is better!

If I don't use drugs and start to talk about my problems, I will slowly start to feel useful to others and myself.

Sanity 365

Daily Reminder
January 19

Think about it!

We thought drugs meant happiness, and for a short time, perhaps they did. As time went on, drugs meant problems, but we tried to convince ourselves that

LIAR

they still meant happiness. Even after jail, suicide attempts, and loss of family and people who cared, we still believed we could find happiness in drugs!

Trying is good! Doing is better!

We experimented with drugs long enough and did not find happiness. Are we now ready to try something that will?

19

Daily Reminder
January 20

Think about it!

When we are bored or depressed, usually we are only thinking about "poor me." It is good to think about our problems, but we also have to do something

ACTION

about them. Just talking to someone will bring relief. The problems may still be there, but they won't seem as deadly! I have problems, but people have answers!

Trying is good! Doing is better!

You will never find out how to do something if you don't ask. How sick must I get before I ask for help? Don't waste any more time!

Daily Reminder
January 21

Think about it!

FOCUS

If we are not happy clean, we will once again try to get happy stoned. For some reason, we believe that every day should be problem-free. That is not reality. We had more problems when we were stoned—we just refused to see them. We always blamed others, not ourselves for our problems, which gave us an excuse not to deal with them.

Trying is good! Doing is better!

I have problems—my friends have answers! Am I ready to listen to their answers and try their advice?

Daily Reminder
January 22

Think about it!

Normal people see us as idiots! Our problem is we think we're okay and they are idiots! Until we can see what we are doing to ourselves, we will stay messed up.

CONNED

We are like hamsters on a wheel, doing the same thing over and over and going nowhere. When will we get off the wheel and on the road to somewhere?

Trying is good! Doing is better!

Garbage in, garbage out! When we start to put something good into our lives, we will get good results. What good can I put into my life?

Daily Reminder
January 23

Think about it!

Our minds and bodies have become messed up because of the garbage we have put into them. To stop the

BEGIN
mess, we have to stop the garbage. This is the only way to begin. We cannot continue to use and still expect to get better. You cannot be sick and well at the same time! Am I tired of being sick?

Trying is good! Doing is better!

How many times have I decided to change, but did nothing? If we drop drugs, but don't replace them with something better, we will soon pick up drugs again!

Daily Reminder
January 24

Think about it!

CLEAN UP

If you have a barrel half full of rotten apples and fill it up with good apples, you'll soon have a full barrel of rotten apples. If we try to put good things into our lives without taking out bad things, we will end up the same way. It is painful to get rid of the garbage, but we must if we want results in our lives

---

Trying is good! Doing is better!

We must stop completely at the stop sign, check all three ways, and then decide which way to go! Have I decided where I'm going?

Daily Reminder
January 25

Think about it!

When you know where you want to go, it is much easier to get there! There are many roads we've gone down and still didn't get the results we wanted. We would turn around and go down another with the same results. If we drive the same old car, we will always be disappointed.

LOST

In other words, we must change who we are if we are to get better results.

Trying is good! Doing is better!

If we do a little work, we will feel a little better. If we do a lot of work, we will feel a lot better. How do I want to feel—a little better or a lot better?

Daily Reminder
January 26

Think about it!

Some people appear to get clean fairly easily! Others battle day after day and then go back to using. No one knows for sure why some people can accept the help and others can't. The one fact we do know is that if we are to live clean and happy, we must accept help and change our thinking and living habits!

CHANGE

Trying is good! Doing is better!

Once our attitude becomes one of gratitude, it's as if our lives are ignited by a rocket fuel! We begin to reach the potential we were created with!

Daily Reminder
January 27

Think about it!

Going one minute, one hour, and one day without drugs is where we must begin. The fear, confusion, and physical sickness will attempt to drive us back to using.

GUTS

If we have made up our minds that we want to get clean, then with the help of our friends, we can fight off the temptation to go back. At the beginning, each minute seems like a day. We can make it. How much courage am I willing to show?

Trying is good! Doing is better!

We must believe our friends who are helping us to win and not all the false promises of drugs that will cause us to lose again!

Daily Reminder
January 28

Think about it!

No matter how long we are clean, the animal called addiction will try to get us using again. This is something we must be on guard against even after many years! When we start living in our heads instead of our guts, our egos can begin to tell us we're cured. That is when we are in danger of returning to drugs. Am I living in my head or my guts?

WRONG MESSAGE

Trying is good! Doing is better!

Our heads can convince us that someone as smart as us could not possibly be an addict. Am I that smart?

Daily Reminder
January 29

Think about it!

When I was finally convinced that to use was to die, accepting help became much easier! The more I changed, the more I wanted to change. Discovering and changing the defects that kept me a loser for years became the most rewarding thing in my life! This is not as easy as popping a pill, smoking a joint, or sticking a spike in your arm, but it's more rewarding!

THE PRIZE

Trying is good! Doing is better!

Am I content to go day by day not using, or do I also want to live a real life and get the rewards that come with it?

Daily Reminder
January 30

Think about it!

If you are an addict, the clean life is the only hope you have of ever being a success! Many people over time did not believe this to be true and went back to using. They ended up in jail, in mental hospitals, or dead. Some survived; that was all they did. They don't really live a happy, successful, giving life. There has to be more to life than just being clean!

HAPPY CLEAN

Trying is good! Doing is better!

When we try to help another person reach his or her potential, we begin to understand what life is about!

Daily Reminder
January 31

Think about it!

When we are clean for a little while, we may start to look down our noses at other people. We may think perhaps we aren't addicts because we're not as bad off as some others. Perhaps you aren't as bad off as others, but if you go back to drugs, you will end up worse than the people you are comparing yourself with.

COMPARING

Trying is good! Doing is better!

If you compare yourself to others, you could become vain or bitter. There are always people who are worse off or better off!

February

**Daily Reminder
February 1**

Think about it!

Patience! Over the years, I have been able, with the help of God and other people, to make a lot of progress in this area. Almost every drug we used was designed to give instant results. That's what we expected when we used! The clean life doesn't usually work that way, so having to wait takes some getting used to. Deciding when I should wait and when I should act often causes me problems! That is when I need some prayer and human advice!

TIME

Trying is good! Doing is better!

I often get different opinions from different people! This adds to the confusion! I must take all this advice to God, and when my guts feel good, go with that decision!

Daily Reminder
February 2

Think about it!

Drugs are something we do until we grow up! For some of us, that took longer than it should have! If we are in our thirties when we get clean, it's harder on the ego to admit we don't really know how to live without dope. The people who do recognize they are shy on life skills are the people who make the most progress toward becoming happy clean. People who deny this fact, if they do stay clean, it is not usually happy clean.

SKILLS

Trying is good! Doing is better!

You may say, "I know people who never did drugs and they have no life skills either!" That's possible, but they don't have to worry about an overdose, murder charge, or mental institution because they don't want to change!

Sanity 365

Daily Reminder
February 3

Think about it!

Many addicts who had success staying clean and then started taking their recovery for granted allowed themselves to be sucked back into the addiction jungle! The self-hate they experience when using after a period of being clean is indescribable. They feel they have let everyone down. They plunge deeper into the world of guilt and insanity. Some are unable to handle the guilt, and they take their own lives! Others, thank God, are reached before they do and get another chance at living!

RETURN

Trying is good! Doing is better!

Bob Marwick is one of those people who was killing himself and through God's grace, is now enjoying being happy clean again. It's possible to make a comeback, folks!

Daily Reminder
February 4

Think about it!

Some people say clothes make the man or the woman! I say that the Main Man makes the man or the woman when we allow Him to! We all stand in the way of our own success. We don't let people or the Main Man interfere in our path to failure! When we do take advice and have some success, we seem to think we are superstars instead of giving the credit to the people with the advice! We then set out to fail again!

LISTEN

Trying is good! Doing is better!

Any success I have experienced has come when I followed God's still, small voice instead of the ego in my own head! Listen to your gut, not your head!

Daily Reminder
February 5

Think about it!

When you were stoned and unhappy, did you blame your dealer? If you are clean and unhappy, should you blame your recovery program or God? Why do we sit in a negative state, waiting for a magic wand to change our lives? Drugs didn't do it, so there is no magic wand! The magic wand happens when we start taking control of our own situation and start getting honest with ourselves, our friends, and God—whatever our understanding of God is! Until then, we will remain unhappy!

BLAME GAME

Trying is good! Doing is better!

How often did you get free dope? No, I mean free dope! No price, no sexual favors, completely free! Oh yeah? Getting happy clean is not free either! It requires work by the person who wants to be happy clean!

Daily Reminder
February 6

Think about it!

I find my ego takes a beating when I realize that all I can handle is today! My brain wants to believe that I can map out the rest of the year and skate to success in everything I do! Smelling the flowers or the coffee just for today, my mind says its okay for the earthlings, but I have too many important projects to complete! Why is it that they never seem to get completed? Whose fault is it? Mine? When I concentrate on living and loving today, I am amazed at my success!

SIMPLE

Trying is good! Doing is better!

Count your blessings today! Start with the fact that you're alive! You are, aren't you? Come on, have a little smile or maybe even a snicker, and then get moving!

Daily Reminder
February 7

Think about it!

Each day we are given a chance to make up for the mess we have made of our lives up until now! A new day, a new life! If you are convinced that drugs will not lead to success, then you must put all your energy into your new way of living. Are you here to change or just until you settle things in court or with your family? Be honest now, or you will regret it later!

MOTIVES

Trying is good! Doing is better!

Sometimes we look for help, not always because we want to get clean. However, if we stay clean long enough, our reasons can change and we will want to be drug-free.

Daily Reminder
February 8

Think about it!

If we have had difficulty staying clean, have we looked at our patterns? Have we stumbled on the same things over and over? What are the things that cause us to give up and go back to drugs? Until we honestly look at these things for what they are, we will once again be dragged out there. We have lived a charmed life up until now, but our luck will eventually run out! Will the next time lead to a graveyard?

DECISION

Trying is good! Doing is better!

Staying clean is a piece of cake once we decide we want to! Until we give in completely, we will have little success! Jump into it!

Daily Reminder
February 9

Think about it!

Have I admitted and accepted that drugs are my master? Do I still think that somehow, someday, I will be able to use drugs in a controlled way? Do I tell drugs when I will use them, or do drugs tell me when I will use them? More than 80 percent of people doing time in jail are there because of drugs. How many times must I go to jail before I accept the truth? One more day in jail is one more lost, wasted day in my life!

LOST

Trying is good! Doing is better!

We often say we will stop using tomorrow, but tomorrow never becomes today! Tomorrow we could be in jail, in a mental institution, or dead! Let's begin today!

Daily Reminder
February 10

Think about it!

At the beginning, we know we need help, but we're not sure if we want help! Each day we stay clean gives us a chance to see ourselves as others see us. We have played so many games in our lives that we don't know who the real us is. Over many years we have tried to pretend we were okay and everyone else was not! To accept what others see is hard, but if we do, we will have swallowed some big chunks of truth about ourselves and be on the road to freedom!

FREE

Trying is good! Doing is better!

Others will see many good qualities in all of us that we do not see. No one is all bad, and you will be shown that as well!

Daily Reminder
February 11

Think about it!

What is my biggest problem today? Whatever it is, I must say it out loud to someone or everyone. If I don't, the problem will get bigger. If I do, I will suddenly discover that it is not as big as I thought! Keeping things inside causes them to grow. We have to start trusting in our friends if we expect to get help. If we could solve our own problems, we wouldn't need help or daily reminders from anyone!

TRUST

Trying is good! Doing is better!

Putting our trust in others can be very scary, but what other choice do we have? Would we rather put our trust in drugs and our friends who are still using?

Norm Sharkey

**Daily Reminder
February 12**

Think about it!

The most important person is the person who is just coming to us for help. That is why our own example is so important. New people will very quickly see if we are real or not! If we are playing games, it won't take them long to see that. They can use us as an excuse to go back out again. We owe it to new people to be real and caring. We must always ask ourselves, "How were people with me when I came in looking for help?"

HONEST

Trying is good! Doing is better!

As time goes on, the people you are meeting will become the best friends you have ever met. These are just not words; this is a fact! Stick around and find out

Daily Reminder
February 13

Think about it!

Today is the most important day of your life! If your thinking is positive today, you'll have a terrific day no matter the problems! Look for a positive way to

POSITIVE
change the problem. Talk to people and ask for their help! Sometimes when you talk about problems, you'll find your own answers

while you are talking. If you don't, then you must listen to others and try to do what they suggest. If there is no answer today, there may be one tomorrow. Keep thinking positive!

Trying is good! Doing is better!

If we have a positive attitude for 365 days, we will be clean and happy for one year. Just think what you can do if you are clean for one year!

Norm Sharkey

Daily Reminder
February 14

Think about it!

To many of us, today is more than Valentine's Day! On this day in 1977, a drug recovery program called Our House was born! It was created for addicts by addicts!

LOVE

Five of us moved into an old, rundown townhouse and tried, with a lot of success, to live a clean, happy, helping lifestyle!

I lost track of the other four people over the years, but I think about them often, and I wish them a happy anniversary, along with hundreds and hundreds of other former residents! How is your day on your day? Are there five people out there with the same idea?

Trying is good! Doing is better!

If you know five people who want the experience of their life, get together and create it! The world needs answers, not problems!

Daily Reminder
February 15

Think about it!

REAL

Honesty! We believe this to be the most important tool in getting and staying clean—honesty with ourselves and others! When we are not honest with others, we begin to feel phony around them and our friendships begin to suffer. Our real friends can tell when we are being phony with them and will, in time, confront us about it. If we do not get real, we will feel a lot of guilt and may use again.

Trying is good! Doing is better!

*I expect my friends to be honest with me,
so I better be honest with them.*

Norm Sharkey

**Daily Reminder
February 16**

Think about it!

Why is it so difficult to be completely honest? How can a little white lie hurt anyone? We have found over time that we are either all or nothing. We go **HELP** to extremes! A small lie becomes a bigger lie and we are back where we started, full of crap! How can we help others to be honest when we are not?

Trying is good! Doing is better!

*One toke, pill, or hit leads to two. One lie leads to two.
If we are to stay content, we must be honest.
If we are not content, we will be stoned!*

Daily Reminder
February 17

Think about it!

DECISIONS

When we decide we must and want to stay clean, we begin to understand how important being honest is for us. We have made some real friends for the first time in many years, and we know we depend on them being honest with us. Trust was not something we could understand because we could not be honest with ourselves.

Trying is good! Doing is better!

Being honest with ourselves and others will lead to people trusting us and us trusting them!

Norm Sharkey

Daily Reminder
February 18

Think about it!

Trust! We cannot expect people to trust us until we can show them we can be trusted. Again we come back to honesty! If we are honest with others, they will begin to trust us. Also, if they are honest with us, we will begin to trust them. It's that simple! Are we ready to start living an honest life?

TOGETHER

Trying is good! Doing is better!

If you are telling someone something and you know it's a lie, simply stop and say, "I'm sorry, I was starting to lie to you! Please help me to be honest!"

Daily Reminder
February 19

Think about it!

Learning to be honest is an ego-busting experience for us! For as long as we can remember, we thought that telling the truth was for fools! We would never get

TRUTH

what we want if we told the truth! We also wanted to impress people with big stories we stole from someone else! In time, we began to believe our own lies.

Trying is good! Doing is better!
---

*When I stop trying to impress people,
I will begin to relax around them and realize
I only have to be who I am.*

Norm Sharkey

**Daily Reminder
February 20**

Think about it!

REAL

Real! This is another benefit we get from being honest! We knew nothing about being real because we used drugs to stay in a fantasyland. We couldn't be honest when we were stoned because honesty didn't impress anyone. The game was who could tell the biggest lie and make it sound real! Real people scared the hell out of us.

Trying is good! Doing is better!

*Starting with one person, see how it feels
to be honest with him or her. You will begin
to see what a friend really is!*

52

Daily Reminder
February 21

Think about it!

If you have one true friend, you have more than most people have. If you think about all the people you know, you will probably realize you don't really know them. That is as much your fault as theirs. You probably have never taken the time to be completely honest with them or they with you. So now how many friends do you have?

FRIEND

Trying is good! Doing is better!

Know the truth and the truth will set you free!
Start being free today!

Daily Reminder
February 22

Think about it!

THINK

George Santayana wrote, "Those who cannot remember the past are condemned to repeat it." That is a fact for addicts. Over time, we seemed to be able to push things out of our memory and convince ourselves they were not so bad. We also told ourselves that this time we would be able to control how much we use!

Trying is good! Doing is better!

Suppose we were able to control our use—how much fun is that? That is like giving an alcoholic two drinks and then cutting him or her off.

Daily Reminder
February 23

Think about it!

Sooner or later, if we live long enough, we will have to honestly look at why we think we need drugs to live! What is missing in our lives that we feel drugs will fix? Drugs will only give a short fix, and then we will need more and more and more! Why do we feel we're not good enough to compete in life without drugs?

FAKE

Trying is good! Doing is better!

If we feel lost and hopeless, we are sitting ducks for drugs. Drugs will only help people who are in that condition. Am I lost and hopeless?

Norm Sharkey

Daily Reminder
February 24

Think about it!

If we are to live a happy, drug-free life, then there are some things we must begin to do! You must try to examine when and why you first started to feel you were not as good as other people. Our heads tell us we are as good as others, and then moments later, it says we're not. We must honestly look at the things that make us feel useless and put them on paper so once and for all we can see them!

FOCUS

Trying is good! Doing is better!

Putting these things on paper is a very important beginning. Now we need to find someone we trust to talk to about them. You will see you are not all bad!

Sanity 365

Daily Reminder
February 25

Think about it!

If you go to the dentist with a toothache, he will say you must have the cavity drilled out and a filling put in. You say to him, "I don't want the pain from the drill. Just fill it." The problem with that is the tooth will still ache. You can't fill the tooth and be free of pain. You must remove the decay.

CLEAN UP

Trying is good! Doing is better!

We used drugs as a painkiller instead of looking and changing what was causing the pain. What can I do about my pain?

Norm Sharkey

Daily Reminder
February 26

Think about it!

When we decided we wanted help, we usually expected fast results, just like drugs gave us! We will get results at the same rate we are prepared to work for them. At the beginning, trusting people is a scary thing. We trusted our dealers when we shouldn't have and many other people who kept us sick. We now must begin to trust real people.

HELP

Trying is good! Doing is better!

Ask people from your group how they were able to trust other people. They will tell you how they did it and who those people were.

Sanity 365

Daily Reminder
February 27

Think about it!

Everyone has a fear of trusting! A stray animal that is starving may only come close to us if we show it some food. It may still think there is a trick and it will **GRAB IT** be caught and beaten if it takes the food. We are not much different at the beginning of our clean life. We must take a chance that there is no trick!

Trying is good! Doing is better!

If we are starving, we must trust and try the food to see there are no hidden costs to us for eating it!

Daily Reminder
February 28

Think about it!

THE LIGHT

Each day we are drug-free, we will begin to understand more about ourselves. We will see that there are many good people in the world. A lot of people in our past tried to steer us right, but we couldn't listen because it went against our drug lifestyle. Can we now see what they were trying to do?

Trying is good! Doing is better!

The drug world and the real world are very different. When we were using, we thought that was real and the real world was plastic. It was exactly the opposite!

Daily Reminder
February 29

Think about it!

Some of us have friends or even brothers and sisters who have found help to get clean! This will make the road to freedom much easier for us to walk. If it worked for them, it can work for you. Listening to them tell how things worked out for them will give you some hope for yourself. For once in your life, perhaps you will be able to show love to your family!

HOPE

Trying is good! Doing is better!

Perhaps there is a history of addiction in your family. By getting help for yourself, you could help the whole family!

March

**Daily Reminder
March 1**

Think about it!

Our families often feel they are to blame for our using. Perhaps in some cases they are, but we can't blame it all on them. If we do, we will not be ready to change the habits and attitudes that kept us high. We must understand that our parents may have had problems, which no one helped them work out. Now you can help them and yourself!

COMPASSION

Trying is good! Doing is better!

We must first look at change and ourselves before we can help others! If we are changing, others will be more likely to listen to us and also change.

Daily Reminder
March 2

Think about it!

Some of us have tried to stop using many times. We did well for a while, but then we stopped taking advice on how to stay clean and went back to using. We must look at the mistakes we made and not repeat them or we will use again. We must decide if we are serious about staying clean! If we are, we will talk about our past mistakes and ask for help to avoid repeating them.

DOING

Trying is good! Doing is better!

There are many people ready to help us, but if we don't follow their advice, we will fall again. Am I ready to apply the advice I am given?

**Daily Reminder
March 3**

Think about it!

We used drugs, used people, and were used by people! As long as we have people to use, we will not get clean. As long as someone will look after us, we will not look after ourselves! We lean on people and on drugs to survive! When people will not let us use them anymore and we are the ones being used, we begin to understand we must get help!

USER

Trying is good! Doing is better!

Am I tired of being a sponge? I have some pride, and I want to be able to stand on my own two feet!

Daily Reminder
March 4

Think about it!

How do we begin to stand on our own two feet? We have hurt many people, so we must decide who will be the first person we can make things right with. We must be real about this or it will not work. Apart from

I'M SORRY

ourselves, who have we hurt the most in our life? If this person refuses to see you or talk on the phone, let him or her know when he or she is ready to listen, you really want to apologize. Keep going on to the next person on your list.

Trying is good! Doing is better!

Most people will be ready to accept your apology.
If some don't, maybe they will in time.
Don't use that as an excuse.

Sanity 365

Daily Reminder
March 5

Think about it!

Some people on your list may also be users who are not ready to get clean and are using you as an excuse to get stoned. If that is the case, go on to the next person.

CONTINUE

There is a lot of work to do; don't let people delay you. We have spent a long time messing up ourselves and others, so it will take time to straighten things out! The more people we apologize to, the better we will feel.

Trying is good! Doing is better!

You may find those people you have hurt may also apologize to you for something they did to you. This will give you a chance to forgive them.

Daily Reminder
March 6

Think about it!

The more we change, the better we feel. We become less nervous because we are cleaning up our past instead of making it dirtier! When we are staying clean, we don't have to look over our shoulders all the time.

RELAX

We can begin to look people in the eyes. We begin to understand what the word peace means. Little by little, the expression Higher Power begins to make sense!

Trying is good! Doing is better!

When we forgive ourselves and others, God starts to become a part of our day, and we begin to be a part of His day!

Sanity 365

Daily Reminder
March 7

Think about it!

HONESTY

If we are not ready to admit that drugs have us beat, we will go back to using. This fact is not easy for us to accept. We look at other people who seem to be able to use and get by, so we feel we should be able to do the same. If we take a closer look, we see these people are not doing so well either! Perhaps if you talked to them, they would tell you they wish they could find a way to stop using!

Trying is good! Doing is better!

Am I ready to die rather that admit that drugs have me beat? Is there not more to life than drugs?

Daily Reminder
March 8

Think about it!

As was mentioned earlier, helping others makes us feel useful. Usually when we are bored, it is because we are looking for excitement. We are the type of people who use people instead of helping people! When we try to help people, we begin to feel good about ourselves. When we try to use people, we feel the opposite. We must feel good about ourselves to stay clean, so we must give instead of take.

GIVE

Trying is good! Doing is better!

Many people do not yet know that drugs are keeping them from living. We do know, so we must tell them what we have learned!

Sanity 365

Daily Reminder
March 9

Think about it!

Some days, we think things are taking too long to turn around for us. We want everything to happen quickly in our life! We are used to sticking a spike in our arm and having all our problems go away. Our problems seemed to go away, but they always came back again. In our drug-free life, we are doing the hard work that will get rid of the problems for good. Some problems may be harder to move than others, but they, too, will go if we persist!

SLOW DOWN

Trying is good! Doing is better!
---

*Each morning, we should look at ourselves
in the mirror and ask if we are solid people or soft crap!
Which is it today?*

71

Norm Sharkey

Daily Reminder
March 10

Think about it!

When we decide to get clean and change, we must stop hiding from life and people. If we have problems with others, we must be ready to face them, our family, the law, other users, our dealers, etc. We will not be able to straighten this mess out by wishing it would go away. We must stand on our feet, and with the help of our friends, we can start to clean things up. Am I up to it?

SOLID

Trying is good! Doing is better!

How far down the road to hell must we go before we get help? As we get closer to the end, the smell is sickening!

Daily Reminder
March 11

Think about it!

We like to think we were able to survive because we were so smart! The fact is, many people covered our tracks many times. Sometimes our using friends helped us; sometimes our family or sometimes the law gave us a break. We still thought it was our smarts that got us through. When no one was ready to stick his neck out for us anymore, we saw the game was over. We had no choice but to get help. The end was here!

CORNERED

Trying is good! Doing is better!

The end of one life is the start of another.
We must do things differently in this new life or
we will go back to the old one!

Norm Sharkey

Daily Reminder
March 12

Think about it!

We must begin our day by thinking positive thoughts. I am going to have a good day today! What must I do to have a good day? I must talk honestly about my thoughts. When we think too much and don't talk, **TALK** we end up in trouble. It's called "stinkin' hinking'!" We think, If I talk about it, what difference will it make? Just try, and you will find out. We don't know until we try! It will work!

Trying is good! Doing is better!

Believe others who have gone before you.
The results will start to show if you keep at it!

Daily Reminder
March 13

Think about it!

Thinking positively and then putting that thinking into action will bring amazing results. Most of our lives, we have been followers. We let drugs do the leading down the road to hell. We often thought about changing directions, but drugs kept leading. Other people could see our potential if we got clean, but we could not. Once you start to think and act in a positive way, you will discover what other people have seen for years. Don't miss out!

LEADER

Trying is good! Doing is better!

What are some of the dreams you have had but could not reach? Talk about them and reach for them!

Norm Sharkey

***Daily Reminder*
*March 14***

Think about it!

Successful people have a dream, and then they do whatever has to be done to make that dream a reality. They keep their eyes on the dream regardless of how many times disappointment tells them to give up. These people believe they can do it, and they do! Most of us try a few times and then convince ourselves that the dream was impossible or stupid to begin with. We don't have the determination to stay with it to a successful end. No wonder so many of us go back to using again!

DO IT

Trying is good! Doing is better!

Martin Luther King had a dream and had his life taken away because of it, but he saved so many more lives pursuing it! Completing our dreams will make us complete! Go for it! You might just save your own life trying to reach your dream.

Daily Reminder
March 15

Think about it!

This book is for people who are tired of being losers! This book will help you look at yourself, but it will not make you a winner without a lot of blood and guts on your part. The purpose of this book is to challenge you each day to stay the course. Today you must decide you are not a wimp who needs drugs to cope with life! You must stop using people and situations as excuses for failure. It is, after all, your life!

GO

Trying is good! Doing is better!

Get out of that bed and get going! Today is the day you begin changing you! Go! Go! Go!

Norm Sharkey

Daily Reminder
March 16

Think about it!

Real pride is, of course, the opposite of ego that kept us stoned! Real pride allows us to get up in the morning and head off to school or work knowing we are not great, grand, and wonderful but human beings ready to have a positive, productive day! When we change the negatives in our lives, we begin to love ourselves. As a result, we begin to understand what real pride is, and others also see the change.

REAL PRIDE

Trying is good! Doing is better!

The more we are open and honest with people, the more we will connect with God as we understand God. Know the truth, and the truth will set you free!

**Daily Reminder
March 17**

Think about it!

One day, we all had to recognize that the reason for our lack of success was because we were looking for a free ride through life! We didn't even want to pay for the lottery ticket! We were saying to life, "Buy the ticket for me, and make sure it is the grand prize winner! If I can't win it all, I don't want to win anything!" We are bored with life, but we never seem to realize that we can do something about that besides getting stoned!

WORK

Trying is good! Doing is better!

Who is responsible for my life? Is it my parents, my wife, my husband, my girlfriend, my boyfriend, the government? No, no, and no again! I am!

Daily Reminder
March 18

Think about it!

"Responsibility—this is for everyone except poor me, right? I am not responsible for anything that happened to me or anyone else in the world! It's everyone else's problem. I am addicted. Therefore, I am blameless! I cannot be held responsible as long as I'm using, right? Everyone knows addicts are not responsible. I am just living up to the image of an addict! There, the perfect copout!" After those talks with yourself, you went out and got stoned before someone had a chance to blow holes in your excuse.

NOT GUILTY

Trying is good! Doing is better!

There is nothing more pathetic than a human who blames the world for his or her problems! Thanks to God that I lived long enough to see this was me! Is it you?

Daily Reminder
March 19

Think about it!

Ego also controls our lives! Our ego will not let us ask for help. Instead, we crawl along on our hands and knees through life. We could be standing tall and racing through life if we would only ask for help! **HELP** Ego has killed many drug addicts. We think people will look down on us if we say we need help. People have known for a long time now that we are lost. It is obvious to everyone except us! Reach out!

Trying is good! Doing is better!

When you ask for help and change your life, then you will discover what real pride is like! People will also be proud of you!

Daily Reminder
March 20

Think about it!

If you are still using and reading these reminders each day, you are a masochist! If you do want help to change, you can also be fulfilled! As we have mentioned several times before, there are different strokes for different folks! If what you are reading here screws your head up, try reading something else. Don't just say this is crap and go out and get stoned!

BE HONEST

Trying is good! Doing is better!

Chewing and digesting the truth about my life was a very difficult thing to do. Many times, I threw up! I didn't realize, however, that it was my only hope of success!

Daily Reminder
March 21

Think about it!

Being real! That was one thing we couldn't possibly know anything about because we used everything we could get our hands on to avoid being real! For some of us, our parents were real, so when we finally stopped using, some of the advice they tried to give when we were kids suddenly made some sense! The advice I received and gave on the street was not advice that could make a person successful, loving, or real! It was just the opposite!

RUNNING

Trying is good! Doing is better!

Facing reality, pain, disappointments, and rejection are all things we have to learn to do without running for dope! If you face these things clean, you'll get stronger! If you don't, lace up the track shoes!

Daily Reminder
March 22

Think about it!

FEAR

Fear controlled our life like a giant toothache! Unless we were stoned, we were worried. The minute we came down, fear was there facing us, and we had to get stoned again! The fear was not there by chance. We have ripped many people off, we have cheated on our friends and family, we have lied to our bosses, and we have cheated on exams! We could not run away from ourselves! We were getting close to insanity! Fear causes insanity!

Trying is good! Doing is better!

Our only hope of surviving is to get honest with our families, our friends, and ourselves. That is the answer to fear!

Sanity 365

Daily Reminder
March 23

Think about it!

When we continue with our thoughts about fear, we see very clearly that we cannot be free from fear unless we are honest! The honesty starts with oneself! We thought we could avoid that with drugs! For a while we may have, but we had to start using more and stronger drugs as the fear carried on! Finally, there was no escape! As the expression goes, "You can run, but you can't hide!" We can get locked up, kill ourselves, or get murdered, or we can get clean! These are our choices! Fear delivered us to this!

CHOICE

Trying is good! Doing is better!

Being honest! That is enough to bring on more fear, right? However, we have to start somewhere, someday! What about now?

Daily Reminder
March 24

Think about it!

If we hope to stay content and happy for the rest of our days, we must be clean and free of fear! We have decided that one way to be free of fear is to be honest! Today! We may see being honest for the rest of our lives as an impossibility. It probably is, but we can be honest today! Telling someone, for instance, "I don't have your money" is better than saying, "I'll have it tomorrow" when you know you won't! Reality! Remember? Talk to them!

FREE

Trying is good! Doing is better!

Instead of facing people we owe money, we avoid them! We don't return phone calls, and we don't answer letters! We think somehow it will all look after itself! It will—it will get worse!

Sanity 365

Daily Reminder
March 25

Think about it!

A DEAL

On June 6, 1971, I got on my knees and asked God to save me from what I thought was a heart attack! I said that if He would help me, I would stay clean for the rest of my life! He did, and so far I have kept my word! I have had many problems since then, but I have never used drugs! I believe God took the addiction away. I believe that as long as I do His will for me, I will remain clean and happy!

Trying is good! Doing is better!

God's will for me is very simple: love God, love myself, and love others! No big mystery! Very simple indeed!

Daily Reminder
March 26

Think about it!

I said I've had many problems since I've been clean, but I have had many, many, many more problem-free, contented, happy days than problem days! If we are honest with ourselves and others, the results will be good days! Part of loving me is being honest with myself! Part of loving God is being honest with God! Part of loving others is being honest with others! If we can do this every day, the problems we have will be easily dealt with.

HONEST

Trying is good! Doing is better!

One little white lie, as they are sometimes referred to, starts an avalanche in our life! When will we finally understand that?

Daily Reminder
March 27

Think about it!

PROMISES

Open and honest! Open and honest! Open and honest! We say and hear these words every day. How is it possible that one minute we are talking about open and honest and in the next minute, we are out doing dope? Talking openly and honestly is easy! Doing it is the thing! Addicts can talk, talk, and talk. Action in a positive direction is something we try to avoid! We made promises for years about all the things we would show people. They were just words! Come on!

Trying is good! Doing is better!

If you ever wonder why people don't hear you anymore, just look at the promises you made that were just air!

Daily Reminder
March 28

Think about it!

Drugs are a power greater than we are! When we used, we got stoned! We are either clean or stoned. There are times when we need help and people may not be available. We must reach out to some Higher Power! **POWER** This power can be Allah, Buddha, God, Jesus, or whomever you choose. If you ask people who are having success in staying clean, they will tell you they have developed a relationship with a Higher Power! Try it!

Trying is good! Doing is better!

The one advantage in having a Higher Power to turn to is that your Higher Power is always there no matter when or where you are!

Sanity 365

**Daily Reminder
March 29**

Think about it!

If we are not serious about staying clean and changing, some things we are reading in this book will make us want to throw it out the window. When we are only playing games, we don't want to hear anything that makes us look at ourselves! This book will help people who are serious and upset people who are not! If you are not sick of the way you have been living, reading this book won't change anything for you. You need action!

SERIOUS

Trying is good! Doing is better!

*If you are sick and you drink poison, will you get well?
That's what it's like every time you do drugs!*

Daily Reminder
March 30

Think about it!

Have we got your attention yet? Do you understand that there is more to getting better than just giving up dope? Many of us have stopped using for a week or more, but we didn't change our thinking or living habits. We simply stopped taking poison! If we can't or won't see the damage we have done to ourselves and others and be prepared to do something about it, we will go back to using! Guaranteed! It's just a matter of time—tick, tick, tick, tick!

CHANGE

Trying is good! Doing is better!

Why is it that the people who are using are so smart and people who are staying happily clean are so stupid? Grow up!

Daily Reminder
March 31

Think about it!

Many people give in to drugs one day too soon! Even if life is a bummer today, it could change tomorrow or even this afternoon. Regardless of your age, you have faced many battles in your life. Why do you not think you could face one more? Instead of using the coward's way out, give someone a call! Drugs will not make the problem any better. Drugs will make the problem worse—guaranteed! Drugs are for losers, and you're not a loser! Give yourself a break!

LIVE TODAY

Trying is good! Doing is better!

Apart from dulling your brain so you don't have to face the problem, when have drugs ever changed things for the better?

April

Daily Reminder
April 1

Think about it!

April Fool's was our day! Was there ever a time in your life when you felt you were worth anything? If there was, you need to return to that place in your mind! You don't need to physically return but mentally and emotionally! From that point, you need to rebuild your life using positive methods, not artificial methods like drugs! You must start to build your future on solid ground! It is time to start being honest with yourself and others! This will not be easy after years of being a liar! Start now! Now! Now!

NO FOOL

Trying is good! Doing is better!

Honesty! That is the scariest word in English or any other language to an addict! Drugs are the biggest liars because they don't deliver what they promise!

Daily Reminder
April 2

Think about it!

Honesty! You may be different, but the biggest reason I felt worthless was because I thought everyone could see what a liar I was! I tried to believe my own lies and pretend I was who I wanted people to think I was! The only people who would accept me were other liars like me! We stole each other's lies and laid them on other new liars! In this world, there are always new liars to meet, so I just got sicker!

LIAR, LIAR

Trying is good! Doing is better!

When we remove drugs from our lives, lying to ourselves becomes a lot harder. When we stop hanging around with liars, we have to start getting honest or go back to the liars!

Daily Reminder
April 3

Think about it!

Victory is success in any contest or struggle! Staying clean today is victory over drugs—just for today! Being clean today, being happy today, being successful today, being a good human being today—that is victory today! We spend too much time looking back at our messed-up past and worrying about our scary future! When was the last time you really enjoyed the day you were living? If you live well today, you can make sure that your past does not become your future!

WIN

Trying is good! Doing is better!

Today, my friend, is the most important day of your life! If you really believe that, it will turn out to be a super day for you

Daily Reminder
April 4

Think about it!

When was the last time you went through a whole day without telling a lie of some sort? Lying has become such a habit that it just comes naturally for us! If you're serious about changing, why not start today? It won't be easy because we depended on our lies and stories to get the odd free stone! We now have decided we want to earn anything we get! What we get, we must get honestly! This means telling the truth as well as not stealing!

STOP

Trying is good! Doing is better!

We tried to give the world the image that we were solid— yeah right! About as solid as diarrhea!

Daily Reminder
April 5

Think about it!

When did our problems start with honesty? Mine started when I discovered I could get something or get away with something if I lied. I was very young when I discovered this, so I became a liar very early in life. I had to cover one lie with another, so I became a very skillful liar. Wanting to impress other liars like myself, I would tell a lie if it sounded better than the truth!

Trying is good! Doing is better!

When you get into recovery, you will see that when it comes to lying, you are among professionals! Beware!

Norm Sharkey

Daily Reminder
April 6

Think about it!

We say we believe that if we use again, we will get locked up, go insane, or die! If we really believe that, why do we use again? Perhaps we feel we have another chance to experiment with drugs. What is there to see or feel that we have not already seen or felt? Why do we feel we cannot face life without drugs? Are we that weak and useless?

FIREPROOF

Trying is good! Doing is better!

When was the last time you started something and finished it? Did you feel good when you did? Try staying clean and sticking with it!

Sanity 365

Daily Reminder
April 7

Think about it!

How long we are clean is not as important as how clean we are! We may have many years of drug-free living, but if we haven't changed our attitudes and behaviors, we will still act and think like addicts who are still using! Talking about people negatively when they are not present, throwing temper tantrums when we don't get our own way, acting selfishly with our friends and family—these are the normal habits of active drug addicts! Is that me?

FAKE

Happy birthday, Rosemary!
Trying is good! Doing is better!

*If I want to get the benefits of a drug-free life,
I have to look at myself very carefully every day!
How do I measure up today?*

Daily Reminder
April 8

Think about it!

When I see something I don't like in other people, instead of talking about them behind their backs, I should ask myself, "Am I like that?" If I am honest, I probably am or have been exactly like the other person! This gives me an opportunity to change my behavior and maybe even help that other person to see what he or she looks like! I acted like a goof for years because no one cared enough to tell me to my face. I know now that many people said it behind my back to others. That didn't help me much!

OPEN

Trying is good! Doing is better!

I can't be a phony! I may be able to help someone see who he or she is if I tell him or her how full of crap I was!

Sanity 365

Daily Reminder
April 9

Think about it!

We must learn to love ourselves in order to be able to love others, and we must love others if we are to be loved in return. You can't hate people and expect people to love you. How do we begin to love ourselves? **LOVE ME** We start by being honest with ourselves and others about our past and present. We clean up our past and then on a daily basis continue being honest with ourselves and our friends. If you're serious about loving yourself, this is how you start!

Trying is good! Doing is better!

The reason we fail is we do nothing with good advice. If we want to be winners, we need to use the good advice.

Norm Sharkey

Daily Reminder
April 10

Think about it!

When I became serious about changing and staying clean, I began to see me in other people! I used to think, I'm glad I'm not like them, and then I thought, My God, I am exactly like them! I don't want to be like that anymore, so I better find out how to change! I wanted to show the image of a good, loving person to the world, but when I was alone, I hated almost everyone I knew.

HELP

Trying is good! Doing is better!

When we hate, we are not very good company, especially for ourselves! When will I change the bad company I am keeping?

Daily Reminder
April 11

Think about it!

As long as I think, I only have to start doing drugs and I'll be okay, I will not be in a big hurry to change who I am inside! I used drugs to begin with because I did not think I was good enough to enjoy life as I was! Why then do I think I can now enjoy life without drugs? Am I not still the same person I was before I started using? I'm not; I'm worse! So I must give up drugs and start changing who I am if I want to enjoy life!

CHANGE

Trying is good! Doing is better!

It's amazing how easy changing is when the alternative is death! It sure did motivate me! Perhaps you don't need that motivator!

Norm Sharkey

Daily Reminder
April 12

Think about it!

Dishonesty is bad for the soul. This is definitely a fact in our everyday happiness! If we walk around worried whether or not we will get caught in a lie, we will not be relaxed or content. In our day-to-day living, we have enough things to deal with. Having to worry about what we did or said should not be one of them. Anything that bothers our souls (inner self) has to be removed. Honesty is the way!

PARANOID

Trying is good! Doing is better!

Try going from the time wake up to bedtime being completely honest and see how you feel just before you drift off to sleep!

Sanity 365

Daily Reminder
April 13

Think about it!

Perhaps all this talk about changing is more than I was expecting when I said I wanted help! Maybe I just wanted to get the heat off for a while, not become a saint! Maybe I just wanted some help in court to avoid jail, get the old lady or old man back, or get the kids out of Children's Aid. Was that what I meant by wanting help? That was the help I settled for many times in my life; when does it all stop?

TOUGH

Trying is good! Doing is better!

The beat goes on! It's the other way around, isn't it?

Norm Sharkey

Daily Reminder
April 14

Think about it!

People tell me I can do anything I want to in my life! The question is, what do I want to do? Besides being a superstar billionaire, which I have been many times in my dreams, what can I do that is possible and real? I have discovered I can accomplish almost anything if I'm ready to pursue it to completion! I have (like many other addicts) started numerous projects and given up on them. It's time to cross the finish line!

FINISH

Trying is good! Doing is better!

At the beginning of my recovery, I was very scattered. One day at a time, the confusion gets less as I get honest!

Daily Reminder
April 15

Think about it!

The secret to a contented, clean life is in being open and honest with everyone in your home and work life today. Just today! We lose sight of today when we look too far into the future. We begin to worry about next month or next year, and we forget to love our family today!

TODAY

We need our family and our family needs us, so we must concentrate on their needs as well as our own—today!

Trying is good! Doing is better!

Tomorrow will look after itself if we live well today.
Am I being open, honest, and loving today?

Daily Reminder
April 16

Think about it!

I didn't realize I didn't have to be a superstar. I thought everyone expected that of me. This was a difficult image to live with—having to be perfect in everything I did. Can you imagine that? Yes? That's why

IMAGE

drugs were a perfect fit for me. When I was stoned, I was a superstar. When I came down, I was not! That's why I wanted to be stoned all the time. I finally have had to settle for being an ordinary superstar.

Trying is good! Doing is better!

Persistence is one thing I should be good at!
I persisted on being stoned right to the end!
Why can I not persist now that I'm clean?

Daily Reminder
April 17

Think about it!

I had become a hopeless whiner! No one cared! Everyone was out for himself! The rich get richer, and I get poorer! Poor me! I was not a happy face very often.

NEGATIVE

If anyone wanted to talk about how terrible life was, I was the expert! I was a walking rain cloud! I was positively negative!

Does that remind you of anyone? I am very fortunate to have found people who told me how and showed me how to grow up. Yahoo!

Trying is good! Doing is better!

I am not disabled, but I should be considering what I did to my mind and body! Someone has something for me to do!

Norm Sharkey

Daily Reminder
April 18

Think about it!

For anyone reading this who was clean for some time and decided to use again, what were you hoping to get by using? What was the hopeless situation you felt you needed to escape from? If you are once again clean and want to stay that way, you'll have to honestly answer these questions or you will use again and again! We all have to remember that we cannot escape from ourselves, for better or for worse!

DON'T RUN

Trying is good! Doing is better!

Try to remember some of the best times you had drug-free and look at what you were doing at that time. You must re-create those times!

Sanity 365

Daily Reminder
April 19

Think about it!

One of my biggest problems is dealing with problems! When I was stoned, I simply dealt with problems by getting more stoned! That was the end of problem until I came down, and I usually had created a few more by then. Who cares? Get stoned again! That was my problem-solving solution! I discovered when I got clean that I had to find a new way to solve problems! Since I had no experience in problem solving, I finally started to ask people who did! I got answers—good answers!

HELP

Trying is good! Doing is better!

Just like me, stop pretending you know what to do! I was a kid in an adult body! I needed to ask the grownups.

Daily Reminder
April 20

Think about it!

One statement I am very wary of hearing is, "You are very smart and knowledgeable." This is followed with, "I believe you can help me!" Immediately, my ego is boosted and I begin to think I am the next messiah! It is something I must continually watch for! I can only help you with answers I have found for my own problems! I will tell you that the answers I have may not be your answers. You are free to try them, but if they don't work, try something else!

EGO

Trying is good! Doing is better!

*If I am serious about finding an answer,
I will continue to ask and search until I do!*

Daily Reminder
April 21

Think about it!

When we first used drugs, we discovered drugs could do for us what we were not prepared to do for ourselves. Drugs relaxed us! Drugs made us feel smart! Drugs allowed us to fit in with the crowd! To feel these things, all we had to do was buy some drugs! In other words, we would buy happiness! To develop happiness ourselves would require effort in changing who we were. Drugs, we thought, were easier and quicker!

EASY?

Trying is good! Doing is better!

The easy way is not always the best way.
The easy way can often lead to jail or death!

Daily Reminder
April 22

Think about it!

Most of the problems I have or I think I have today I have created myself! This is a big turn around for me. When I was stoned or first got straight, I thought other people were my problem! No one understood me.

PROBLEMS

Right? Today when a problem shows up, I may at first say, "Fuddle duddle" or something the same as that, but over the years, I have realized the problem has solutions! What can I learn from this problem?

Trying is good! Doing is better!

*Sometimes the solution may not come right away!
Perhaps the lesson to be learned is patience!*

Sanity 365

Daily Reminder
April 23

Think about it!

GRATITUDE

Being grateful is, without a doubt, the greatest gift I or any other addict can receive! Until I found gratitude, I had no continuous success staying clean! I did not see being drug-free as something valuable! It was just something society and my family were imposing on me! As a result of this kind of attitude, I would end up on the street again. When I came close—too close—to death and asked for help, I discovered gratitude!

Trying is good! Doing is better!

Being grateful makes staying drug-free a piece of cake! With gratitude in my heart, I know I can find life's answers to any and all problems! Guaranteed or my money back!

Norm Sharkey

Daily Reminder
April 24

Think about it!

Critics may say that regardless of how loving and respectful you are with your children, they still may turn to drugs. I do not for a moment believe that. I've not seen anyone who has found love and respect from their parents trade that in for drugs. Drugs, love, and respect do not connect! Drug use brings the exact opposite results to love and respect. We do not love or respect anyone, including ourselves, when we are using.

BLAME GAME

Trying is good! Doing is better!

Perhaps I blame my parents for my drug use.
Who do I blame if my children become addicts?

Daily Reminder
April 25

Think about it!

The addict's most popular game: the blame game! There is an endless supply of people to blame—father, mother, teacher, coach, church, girlfriend, boyfriend, boss, other workers, and on and on!

IT'S ME

When I finally ran out of people, and that takes a while, I probably blamed God before I looked in the mirror! Then I began to wonder, is it possible for one person to have gone through all that and survived? Am I dreaming, or did all this really happen to one person?

Trying is good! Doing is better!

Yes, it did happen, and if I lose track of gratitude, it can happen again!

Norm Sharkey

Daily Reminder
April 26

Think about it!

My life has not been a continuous run of problems! Far from it! Like a lot of addicts, I sometimes think something must be wrong if I don't have a problem! Over the years, I have had very few problems that I didn't create myself! I guess I thought if I created a problem, I would have something to practice my problem-solving skills on! Just kidding! It took a while, but I began to understand that life could be fun without dope!

RELAX

Trying is good! Doing is better!

Maybe every day is not a drug high, but the high I do get is real, and it doesn't come from the dealer.

Daily Reminder
April 27

Think about it!

People talk about prevention! Prevention starts at home. A family that is loving, unselfish, and proud of each other is not likely to turn to drugs for answers.

SHOW ME

That does not mean they will not have problems, but they will solve their problems without turning to drugs! Parents have to realize that their children will become mirrors of their parents! What parents see in the mirror is what their children will become. This is where prevention starts.

Trying is good! Doing is better!

The beat goes on! Addicts who have children will quite likely have children who become addicts! They mirror what they see.

Daily Reminder
April 28

Think about it!

I once heard an expression, "Some are sicker than others!" This saying at the time gave me the feeling that I wasn't so bad! It was exactly the thing I should not have heard because it gave me the cop-out I was looking for. I'm okay; I don't have to look at myself or do any changing because I'm not as sick as they are! With that attitude, it was only a matter of time before I was using again! I got as sick as—maybe even sicker than—the others before I could get well!

EXCUSES

Trying is good! Doing is better!

I discovered that looking down my nose at others only brought out more of the "snot" in me!

Sanity 365

Daily Reminder
April 29

Think about it!

Overreacting! We know all about this expression. Perhaps we invented it! Both stoned and clean, we are great examples of this. We are loud, aggressive, and obnoxious or just the exact opposite—meek, calm, and very agreeable! We have a problem finding a middle ground when it comes to behavior! Most of the time, we react to situations the same way as a spoiled child would! If we get our own way, we are like peaches and cream, and if we don't—a tantrum!

QUIT

Trying is good! Doing is better!

The older we are when we get clean, the tougher it is to accept our childish behavior! Suck back the ego and get to it!

Daily Reminder
April 30

Think about it!

We have been told that humans have been created in the likeness of God. If that is the case, when we are born, we are loving and lovable people! Why, then, over time, do we become the exact opposite? I have seen beautiful, loving kids turn into angry, hateful teenagers because of family problems. These kids turn to kids who feel the same way, and then drugs come into play to help them deal with their pain. When you add drugs to an angry person, you have an angry stoned person!

PAIN

Trying is good! Doing is better!

First we must get rid of drugs! Then we must look at and change what caused us to need drugs in the first place!

May

**Daily Reminder
May 1**

Think about it!

When drugs were removed from my life, it was as though all the directions for living were removed! I had depended on drugs for everything, just as a little child depends on her or his parents to guide and comfort him or her. Dealing with situations the way normal people did was something I knew nothing about. Like a stranger in a country without a map, I kept running into dead ends. I began to feel I was absolutely stupid when all I needed was to ask directions!

DEPENDANT

Trying is good! Doing is better!

I finally started to read the directions before I began repairing my damaged life!

Daily Reminder
May 2

Think about it!

Patience! This was a nonexistent word in my life! The only time I was patient was when I was on the nod! Action was the key word in my life, but none of it good! How could I score? Where could I score? How often could I score in the same situation?

USING

The wheels were continually turning. Schemes, schemes, schemes! Without drugs, I was a perfect description of hyper! While waiting for a phone call, I would walk four or five hundred miles in my living room!

Trying is good! Doing is better!

Again, years of instant relief using drugs as a medication didn't equip me very well to practice patience!

Daily Reminder
May 3

Think about it!

The ability to handle money is usually a problem both before and after we stop using drugs! Money to us when we were using was for sex, drugs and rock 'n roll! Other than that, it had very little importance. Cars, clothes, and a place to live were not as important. When we get clean, we are faced with money problems. Remember, if you started to use at twelve or thirteen years old, your experience in money matters will just be like that!

HELP

Trying is good! Doing is better!

We might be wise to get advice about budgets instead of pretending we know what we are doing!

Daily Reminder
May 4

Think about it!

All my life as a using addict, I was able to find fault in almost everyone and everything! I would say things like, "I'm not perfect, but . . ." or "Who are the idiots who thought this up?" I never had any solutions

CRITIC

for the situations, but I sure could be a critic! My life was going nowhere but down, so having a positive attitude was impossible. Today, after years of enjoying a life of living clean, I find it's impossible to be negative!

Trying is good! Doing is better!

*Even when things seem to be upside down,
I know that everything happens for a reason and
everything happens for the best!*

Sanity 365

Daily Reminder
May 5

Think about it!

Anytime I feel tense and anxious, I find that if I examine my thinking, I will once again discover that I have started to live in the past or the future and not in today! Since living today sounds like such a simple way of life, why do I find this to be one of the most difficult things to master? Do I think it means I'm not smart enough to deal with the future? Does it mean I think that people think I'm still just a little child? Ego!

TODAY

Trying is good! Doing is better!

When I think too much, life gets very complicated. That's why I have to slow everything down and live today!

129

Norm Sharkey

Daily Reminder
May 6

Think about it!

No one will promise you a rainbow at the end of every day. There will be nights when you go to bed and toss and turn for a while. If, however, you have been honest and loving that day, you will find the comfort you need to get the sleep you need to face the next day. The most important person to be able to face will be looking at you in the mirror. If you can face that person, everything else will work out.

MIRROR, MIRROR

Trying is good! Doing is better!

*Perhaps we won't get the results we hope for today.
The results may be even better than we hoped for!*

Sanity 365

**Daily Reminder
May 7**

Think about it!

Live today! Why am I so anxious to live tomorrow, next week, next month, or next year? Why do I not appreciate where I am today? My life could perhaps be better today, sure—but it could also be a lot worse! What makes a good day or a bad day? Is it money, sex, friends, a house, or big car? For me, a good day is feeling comfortable inside myself! A good day is if I know that I was honest with myself and everyone around me!

Trying is good! Doing is better!

*Again, I keep coming back to that word honesty!
That is my secret to a comfortable day!*

Daily Reminder
May 8

Think about it!

Still not convinced about the value and comfort of just living for today? You may be like I was. I had never tried living just for one day, so I didn't think it would make any difference! The expression goes, "Don't knock it till you try it." One day I tried it! At many points throughout the day, I found my thoughts drifting into the past or future. When I did, I could feel tension come back to my body and mind! I just kept refocusing on today, and every time that happened, contentment returned!

COOL

Trying is good! Doing is better!

You won't be sold on this idea until you give it a good, solid try. Then you can go to work on someone else!

Daily Reminder
May 9

Think about it!

Drugs gave us the false message that life would be problem-free as long as we were stoned! When we got clean, we seemed to think the world would suddenly be all peaches and cream! There will be problems, but we can deal with them. This will be something new for us because we used to ignore problems when we were stoned! When trying to deal with problems, we may react like little kids do because we have no experience, but with help we can get by.

SOLUTIONS

Trying is good! Doing is better!

Don't think you are alone! We all have problems, but there are answers too! Hang in there! Talk to someone!

Daily Reminder
May 10

Think about it!

How many miles have I tried walking in someone else's shoes? Any at all? It is very easy for me to judge someone, but it takes time and effort to sit down with that person and try to understand why he or she feels the way he or she feels! Most of us are judges, ready to pass sentence! I certainly don't feel good when someone does that to me, so why I am I so quick to do it to someone else? Again I say to myself—grow up!

JUDGES

Trying is good! Doing is better!

I don't find it so difficult to be humble, since I'm perfect and have been all of my life! Not!

Daily Reminder
May 11

Think about it!

Complicating everything can bring on lots of confusion for me! Today I have had a nice, relaxing day because I did not let my head take something simple and straightforward and turn it into a complication!

SIMPLE

As well as just living for today, keeping the day's events simple will produce a nice, worry-free life! Who gave me the job of solving the world's problems today? Whoever it was forgot to leave me the answer sheet! Perhaps I wasn't given that job!

Trying is good! Doing is better!

Have you ever felt like I do? That the future of the world depends on you? I sure hope not!

Norm Sharkey

Daily Reminder
May 12

Think about it!

Perhaps you think we have talked too much about honesty, but without it we are lost! Honesty to us is like the rudder for boat. Without a rudder, the boat is without direction. We are the same without honesty! **DIRECTION** Anything goes! Where we go is back to the drug world and insanity! If we just want to be a little bit honest, then we will just have a little bit of happiness. I'm greedy; I want it all!

Trying is good! Doing is better!

Honesty plus love will begin to show you where good, orderly direction is! You can then stay on the right track!

Sanity 365

Daily Reminder
May 13

Think about it!

I couldn't concentrate on living today until I did something about all my yesterdays! Many people's lives were shattered because of me, and I had to do what I could to make things right with them! I found that everyone I talked to was only too happy to forgive me once they could see I was finally serious about staying clean and changing! These people are some of my biggest fans today! I don't ever want to go back and tell them that I screwed up again!

CLEAN UP

Trying is good! Doing is better!

I sometimes wonder if I could forgive as completely as the people I hurt if the shoe was on the other foot!

Daily Reminder
May 14

Think about it!

Once the past is dealt with, I can begin to live today without constantly looking in my rearview mirror! I began to understand how to plan for the future but also that I could not plan the end results! Plant a garden **WORK** and then water it and weed it and let it grow! Why do I think things are not growing fast enough? One day at a time, they will grow if I do the work of the gardener, right?

Trying is good! Doing is better!

Patience and faith in doing what I have to do today will bring me a bountiful, amazing harvest!

Sanity 365

Daily Reminder
May 15

Think about it!

As we begin to discover love for ourselves, we will begin to discover we can love other people who also think they are not capable of being loved. If we are being open and honest with ourselves and others, **LOVE** we can continue to supply ourselves and our friends the love we all need. Of course, they must do the same for us! It's selfish, perhaps, but we need this love for ourselves and others as much as we need clean air to breathe! Without it, we will use!

Trying is good! Doing is better!

Burn this into your brain: to be free, you must be honest!
We have tried many other things that don't work!

Daily Reminder
May 16

Think about it!

Love, honesty, and living for today! Why do I keep repeating these three things? Because I have found that for me, they are the key to being content, grateful, and drug free! If I am loving people, I usually have it returned to me! If I am honest with people, they will usually be honest with me! I also have found that if I practice these things each day, just for that day, there's not much more I can do for me or for humanity!

GOOD DAY

Trying is good! Doing is better!

That may sound sort of sappy to all you solid people, but how was your day today?

Sanity 365

Daily Reminder
May 17

Think about it!

One of many things I'm grateful for today is the ability to look at my blessings rather than my problems. There are so many people in this world who don't even have enough to eat today! They are trapped in a system that will not allow them to improve their lives! Every day I can improve my mind and body if I'm not too lazy to do it! Nothing stops me from progressing in life but me! I am my only roadblock!

WINNER

Trying is good! Doing is better!

I should have died years ago from drugs! Some of my friends did! I guess the reason you and I didn't die is because we have more work to do!

Norm Sharkey

Daily Reminder
May 18

Think about it!

The difference between winners and losers is that winners learn how to love themselves! That doesn't mean you are better than others; it just means you are better than your old self! Each day is an opportunity

BETTER to become better than your old self! The further you get away from your

old self, the more comfortable you will become with the real you! In other words, you'll start to love the real you! Then you can begin to love others as well!

Trying is good! Doing is better!

Feeling good can become catching. You attract people to you because they want what you have. Share with them!

Sanity 365

Daily Reminder
May 19

Think about it!

I have wasted so much time in my life! I am determined to make today a very productive day! How do I do that? First, I start by thanking God, as I understand God, for a good night's sleep! Then I thank God for all the people, past and present, who have made my life what it is today! Then I ask God for the strength, knowledge, and love to make my own life and anyone I'm involved with better today! Then I get on with the job!

RESCUE

Trying is good! Doing is better!

God and I both have to be involved to get the best results! He can't do it alone, and I can't do it alone.

Daily Reminder
May 20

Think about it!

I used to wake up with problems because I went to sleep with problems! I discovered that if I want the day to start properly, I have to solve any problems within my control before I go to sleep! When I do that, I have a much better chance of starting the next day on solid ground. When I was using, my life was one continuous hangover—not just from drugs but from all the unsolved problems caused by drugs! How about you?

NOW

Trying is good! Doing is better!

Of all the problems you may have or think you have, start with the easiest one and deal with it right now! You can do it! Then deal with the next one!

Daily Reminder
May 21

Think about it!

A man I know stayed clean for a year and then went back to using. I asked him why he decided to use again, and he said, "I just wanted to prove to my family that I could do it." Two days after I spoke to him, he was dead! Somehow, he didn't realize it was himself he had to prove this to, not anyone else. Resentment can kill! It is for me that I must stay clean. It is my life, not theirs. I need not prove anything to anyone but me!

HATE

Trying is good! Doing is better!

If I stay clean today, there is much good I can do for me and for others. If I don't, I lose, and so do they!

Norm Sharkey

**Daily Reminder
May 22**

Think about it!

Many things can cause confusion in my life, but most of the time, I cause my own confusion. I have to look at what I am responsible for and do something about it! I have mentioned many times, the cop out I use is, "It's their fault!" That allows me to do nothing and stay confused! When I deal with my end of the confusion, the sky becomes blue again! I can see the sun! I must deal with me!

CHANGE ME

Trying is good! Doing is better!

I must stop trying to straighten the world out and concentrate on what I have to change! If I'm okay, then I can help!

Daily Reminder
May 23

Think about it!

Am I a caregiver or a caretaker? Am I taking more than I'm giving? Probably! As a person who was very selfish, I recognized some time ago that the more I gave, the more I received! I also recognized that I have to give quality care if I want to receive quality care! Like most people, as my day goes on, the care I give starts to depreciate in quality. By the end of the day, I need a rest! We are not machines! Don't run out of gas!

REST

Trying is good! Doing is better!

Even God rested on the seventh day, so where does that leave us?

Norm Sharkey

Daily Reminder
May 24

Think about it!

There are some of you who will read this little book and are not completely serious about staying clean and changing! We can only pray that you will live long enough to get serious! Not only are you wasting your life being wasted, but you are also tearing the guts out of people who care about you. Why do you hate yourself so much? Is it not time to stop and take a look at you?

FEAR

Trying is good! Doing is better!

If you did to me what I do to me, I'd kill you.
Why are we so eager to beat ourselves up?
Wouldn't you like to be remembered for having done something worthwhile in this life?

Sanity 365

Daily Reminder
May 25

Think about it!

I don't know how many people may eventually read Sanity 365, but my hope is that regardless of how many pick it up, reading this today will make people determined to do something to leave their mark on the addiction community! Recovery for us must mean recovery for others! We can't just take what we get and sit on it! We still may stay clean that way, but we will not really get the full benefits of what this life has to offer!

RECOVERY

Trying is good! Doing is better!
---

*I can do so much! You can do so much!
We can do so much! Let's do it!*

Daily Reminder
May 26

Think about it!

This book is not in competition with any other books on addiction recovery! It is simply one person's experience—both positive and negative—on how to live happily drug-free! The writing is not meant to win any literature awards; it is simply speaking to ordinary people, with drug problems caused by living problems! Usually, the living problems come first. The drugs follow, and the living problems get much worse! So to correct the situation, it seems to me drugs must be eliminated first. Then the living problems!

CALL

Trying is good! Doing is better!

Removing drugs from life was a scary moment, but I made the move and so can you! Call someone now!

Sanity 365

Daily Reminder
May 27

Think about it!

Helping others is a very important part of our recovery; however, we can't forget our families in the rush to help other addicts. Over the years, our families have paid a price for our addiction. We have torn their guts out time after time. They bailed us out, took us to hospitals, talked to employers or school principals for us, and nursed us back to health and sanity. Now it is our turn for payback.

FAMILY

Trying is good! Doing is better!

Staying clean has to be our number-one priority.
Our families should be no less than number one!
Make them that!

Daily Reminder
May 28

Think about it!

Drugs allowed me to run away from myself for years, and then drugs finally forced me to stop and look at myself! Why was I running? What could I do to stop running? When would I stop running? Until I seriously asked myself these questions, I continued running! How about you? Is it time to ask the hard questions, or is your life just great? I have to believe that if drugs were not a problem, you would not be reading these words right now, right?

BREATHE

Trying is good! Doing is better!

I didn't let other people convince me I needed help; I convinced myself! I was lost!

Sanity 365

Daily Reminder
May 29

Think about it!

When I was stoned, I was wasting my life trying to feel happy! I have been clean for quite a few years now, and I still waste a lot of my time! Being happy is not a problem anymore. Also, I am never bored, but I still waste a lot of time doing nothing to help others!

WASTE

I do hope this book will somehow make up for the wasted time! Just putting these thoughts on paper has helped me to feel more useful!

Trying is good! Doing is better!

*Perhaps you feel like I have in the past!
Try putting some of your thoughts on paper!*

Norm Sharkey

**Daily Reminder
May 30**

Think about it!

We go to extremes in most everything we do! Too much seems to be just right! We either do too much of everything or too much of nothing. We are very happy or very unhappy. We are very relaxed or very uptight, we eat too much or not enough, and we have too much sex or none at all. We must find a middle ground for most things, if we are to be content, and also to help the people around us to be content. The only extreme thought we should have is an extreme desire to stay clean.

EXTREME

Trying is good! Doing is better!

Easy does it—but do it! Don't use "easy does it" as an excuse to avoid things that need to be done!

Daily Reminder
May 31

Think about it!

We have many people in this country like me who wasted their own and other people's money and time trying to stay problem-free! We have people going out each day trying to convince people to accept **CONFUSED** help and get off the street! They offer them food, clothing, and shelter, and still, the people choose to live in misery! Then we have people in war-torn or earthquake-devastated countries who have no help for their misery! What's wrong with this picture? What?

Trying is good! Doing is better!

*I have been on both sides of that fence!
The side I'm on now is where I want to stay!*

June

Daily Reminder
June 1

Think about it!

I recognize that a teenager and a senior citizen have different problems and ideas about life, but we all feel pain and discouragement. Each of us has to do what we have to do to feel better! The teenager in a short time may be ready to change, and a senior may die stoned! I believe we all have our own surrender point; some sooner than others, some never. If you are still alive and can't handle any more pain, call for help. Now!

ACCEPT

Trying is good! Doing is better!

This is the day that you could finally start to really live! Please call someone!

Norm Sharkey

Daily Reminder
June 2

Think about it!

When we start feeling sorry for ourselves, the reason is often because we are not trying to help someone else! We don't see that other people have problems that would make ours appear very tiny. When we try to help others, we see our problems are nothing compared to theirs. We need to see that if we are clean, our most important problem is being looked after today. Nothing is so bad that getting stoned won't make it worse. Remember your last day using drugs!

POOR ME

Trying is good! Doing is better!

The good days you have clean are the insurance you can use when you go through some dark days. There will be more good than dark!

Daily Reminder
June 3

Think about it!

To get clean, I had to be scared and sick, really scared and really sick. I mean really! To stay clean, I had to discover gratitude! I don't think I was capable of finding this on my own. I believe this is God's gift to an addict when the addict has finally given up on drugs! I was clean five times before I was given this gift, so I have to believe God saw I was ready! I am grateful today!

FEAR

Trying is good! Doing is better!

I have seen many addicts get stoned again, but I have never seen a grateful addict get stoned!

Norm Sharkey

**Daily Reminder
June 4**

Think about it!

When I was using, I was one of the "world's greatest thinkers"! I didn't do much good thinking, but I did a lot of thinking! Somehow, my thinking continued to lead to problems! When I stopped thinking and just screamed for help, things changed! Then I was told, "Don't think you're not equipped." How right they were! I had to simply follow directions, and the results started to appear. I have discovered that the winners in this game are the doers, not the talkers or the thinkers!

DO

Trying is good! Doing is better!

The things we have to do to reach success are very straightforward! Don't think about it, just do it!

Sanity 365

Daily Reminder
June 5

Think about it!

Being around people who are staying clean is a very large part of our recovery! Talking about how we feel now is as important as talking about our past! If we don't talk about it now, it could turn into our past! **OPEN** Sometimes talking about our past is easier because it is in the past. Our ego may tell us people may not accept us if we tell them what we are thinking and feeling right now. Don't let your ego win!

Trying is good! Doing is better!

Good thoughts lead to good actions! Twisted thoughts lead to twisted actions! What results are you looking for?

Daily Reminder
June 6

Think about it!

In my lifetime, I have disappointed an awful lot of people. Certainly it happened when I was stoned, but it's also happened many times since I've been clean! Sometimes my motives were wrong, and other times I was trying to push people too quickly! Either way, when I get a chance to apologize, it is not always accepted. That's not something I can control. All I can do is let people know I'm sorry. Hopefully one day the people I apologized to will see I meant it!

SORRY

Trying is good! Doing is better!

Don't always look at the mistakes other people are making! Check to see how you're doing!

Daily Reminder
June 7

Think about it!

We were told as children to be honest and straightforward with our parents. When we were, we sometimes got punished. We began to see that there were some things we could be honest about and other things we couldn't! As a result, I learned very early how to become an excellent sneak. This also gave me the tools I needed to become a drug addict! Being sneaky is definitely one of the most important requirements of an addict!

CHANGE

Trying is good! Doing is better!

Changing the habits of a sneak is very difficult to do, but if I want people to be honest with me, I have to change!

Daily Reminder
June 8

Think about it!

If we are without a partner when we get clean, we may go back to our old hangouts looking for someone to hook up with. Since the people in such places are still using, you could feel out of place and intimidated since you are not. In order to relax and perhaps get some sex, you may decide to use again! Are you prepared to die for sex? If we are honest, we may just be prepared to die for sex! We don't think we will—right?

GAMES

Trying is good! Doing is better!

Sex has taken over our lives, just like drugs have. There's no quick, easy fix. We must take it one day at a time, maybe even one minute at a time! If the choice becomes sex or drugs, go with sex, but don't get stoned! Remember! Only if you have no committed relationship or guilt will get you stoned!

Daily Reminder
June 9

Think about it!

When we stop using drugs, every little problem seems as big as a mountain to us—how to socialize without drugs, how to date someone, even what to talk about on a date! I think I was almost as shy as I was on my first teenage date. The lines don't come out as easily without the courage those drugs gave me! At times like that, I began to realize how much my life was run by drugs! Big time!

FEAR

Trying is good! Doing is better!

Learning to live without drugs, making decisions, is a whole new experience, just like starting at a new school!

Norm Sharkey

Daily Reminder
June 10

Think about it!

Some people like to use the phrase making love as though they were about to bake a cake or something—getting all the ingredients into a bowl, turning up the heat, and putting it in the oven! I guess that's one way, but over the years I have discovered if love is not the main ingredient, then all I have is the sex! For many years I was quite happy with that. But when I discovered sex with love, I realized what I had been missing for years! What a difference!

SEX

Trying is good! Doing is better!

The forbidden fruit is what I thought sex was as a teenager! It didn't change as an adult because my thinking didn't change!

Daily Reminder
June 11

Think about it!

When we were using, sex was a very large part of our lives. The more we used, the more sex we wanted. Certain drugs were used to stimulate our sexual appetites! We "gave" people drugs to get them stoned so we could use them for sex! There was always a motive behind our generosity! We were users of people as well as users of drugs. Sex never had any love attached to it. It was simply a conquest and a release. "What's love got to do with it?" was our thinking!

HONESTY

Trying is good! Doing is better!

When we stop using drugs, we have nothing to open the door to sex. That is why a lot of us go back to using again. Just for sex!

Daily Reminder
June 12

Think about it!

I have been talking about sex for the last few days, but what this boils down to is my selfishness as a person, with sex being the end result or the prize at the end of the day! My whole life was not based on how I could make someone else's life better but what I could get out of it! As a result, sex was just one of many things that never seemed to satisfy or give me inner peace afterward! There was no love in my past!

SELF

Trying is good! Doing is better!

I'm sure all of my partners felt the same way, and I really regret that! I hope they have since found love!

Sanity 365

Daily Reminder
June 13

Think about it!

PROTECT

Selfishness is a huge factor in an addict's life, because we will do anything and everything to protect and continue our drug use! Anyone or anything that threatens it becomes the enemy! When family, friends, or employers complained about my drug use, I would move or change jobs! That is how most of us do things. Everything or everyone is removed if they threaten my love (drugs). For some reason, I thought that was very normal! I guess it would be if it were a person I loved and not drugs!

Trying is good! Doing is better!

Today, am I ready to protect the people I love the same way as I was ready to protect drugs? Yes, I am!

Daily Reminder
June 14

Think about it!

I need help, and I'm ready to do whatever I need to do to get clean and stay clean! There are the words that friends and loved ones have been waiting for years to hear. Sometimes the people who say these words mean them, and other times they don't! Some people have said these words many times and ended the next day with a spike in their arm! We say one thing and do another. If only people could believe us!

YES, NO

Trying is good! Doing is better!

Words are only words unless they are backed up by action! Show me; don't tell me!

Daily Reminder
June 15

Think about it!

PROMISES

The promises I made to people when I was using were most likely in the hundreds of thousands or more! None were ever kept. If someone made even one promise to me and didn't keep it, they would live to seriously regret it! Why are the rules okay for me to break, but not someone else? A double standard—I believe that is what it's called! It simply shows what a childish, selfish human being I had become. It gets worse!

Trying is good! Doing is better!

Does this not give you some idea of the work I had to do on me when I stopped using dope?

Norm Sharkey

**Daily Reminder
June 16**

Think about it!

Perhaps people who don't do drugs have some of my unpleasant mannerisms. The difference is that if these defects flare up with them, they are not in danger of killing themselves with dope. I am! Anyone with a drug problem faces that danger! That is addicts have to change and look at themselves on a daily basis! If I don't, am I ready for the alternative? For that reason, now, I don't compare myself to other people. I am who I am, and that's all I am!

CHANGE

Trying is good! Doing is better!

I can handle my problems, but I don't know if I could handle yours! Therefore, I will not try to live your life for you!

172

Sanity 365

Daily Reminder
June 17

Think about it!

Yes, I am ready to get clean! First you have to find me a place to live and not just some lousy room either! I want cable TV with all the bells and whistles (porno) and a fridge full of steak! You'll have to get me a good-paying job with very little work and then call my girlfriend or boyfriend and straighten everything up with them. Those are my conditions! Well—how come you're just staring at me?

LOST

Trying is good! Doing is better!

These are the conditions laid out by people who don't want to get clean! Are you one of them? I'm not!

173

Daily Reminder
June 18

Think about it!

Let us make no mistake—staying clean will require some serious effort! Didn't staying stoned require some? The difference is the ones required to stay clean make me a better human being! Staying stoned makes me worse! What is my choice? For the people who care about us, the choice would be to stay clean! For us, who knows? Does that tell me I might have a mental problem? If I don't know if I want to be sick or well, I think I do have a mental problem!

MENTAL?

Trying is good! Doing is better!

I can now see why people had to treat me like a little boy! That is what I was!

Daily Reminder
June 19

Think about it!

I believe that as an active drug addict, I was not capable of giving or receiving love! I sure wanted all kinds of attention and care, but I didn't know how to respond to it! On the outside, I probably looked like a normal person, but that's as far as the word normal went! Selfish and self-centered was a better way to describe me. Well, over the last few days, I have not painted a very healthy picture of myself. That was me!

UNREAL

Trying is good! Doing is better!

If you think I sound a lot like you, perhaps you have some work to do too! It's not impossible to change! Honest!

Norm Sharkey

**Daily Reminder
June 20**

Think about it!

Now that we have looked in the mirror a bit, what do we plan to do about what we see? Behind us looks like a minefield! What's ahead? Where do we start? Have we had enough insanity? If you're not sure, then

SUCKER

don't waste anyone's time or your own. Get back out into it and enjoy. There still should be someone you can use. You still have all the talk and mannerisms to impress some gullible person! Go for it!

Trying is good! Doing is better!

The world is full of suckers. Drugs discover that every day. Drugs will make you happy while you make someone else miserable!

Sanity 365

Daily Reminder
June 21

Think about it!

Anytime I decided to go back to using dope, it wasn't because I was a happy, together person! The message therefore is, "Drugs appeal to messed up, lost, people!"

SAD That is not the message the drug world wants people to hear, but it is a fact! The drug world wants messed-up people to hear this message: "If you use these drugs, you will be happy and successful and have tons of friends!" Is that your reality, friend?

Trying is good! Doing is better!

I would suggest that if you are happy and successful and have a ton of friends, it's not because you are using dope!

177

Norm Sharkey

Daily Reminder
June 22

Think about it!

If today I am thinking about getting stoned, I can tell you for sure I didn't just start thinking about it today! This thought has probably been bouncing around in my head for some time now! I have lost my gratitude, and I also have stopped looking at what a loser I used to be! Now I am getting ready to become a loser again. I have stopped thinking about helping others and probably even started resenting some of them!

THINK

Trying is good! Doing is better!

When I have arrived at the above situation, drugs are very easy for me to pick up! I have lost my purpose for being clean!

Sanity 365

**Daily Reminder
June 23**

Think about it!

GROW UP

When I was a child, I thought as a child! When I became a drug addict, I still thought as a child! I thought the world was there for me to sample at no cost to me. The people I walked over were not my problem; they should have gotten out of the way. Just because they were trying to hang onto things that belonged to them was no excuse for being in the way. We threw tantrums just like little kids when we didn't get what we wanted! People got hurt!

Trying is good! Doing is better!

*In a supermarket, a child in a tantrum is annoying!
An adult in a tantrum is an addict!*

Norm Sharkey

Daily Reminder
June 24

Think about it!

WORTH

To stay clean, I have said many times that I must be happy and content with myself! I must feel I have a purpose in this life! If I am just going through the motions now, what is the difference if I'm clean or stoned? Stoned, I was just going through the motions of living wasn't I? What I'm saying is I must feel like I'm contributing to life somehow or I won't feel I'm worth anything! People who have some self-worth don't need any additives.

Happy birthday, Trieste!
Trying is good! Doing is better!

*Since I've been clean, when have I felt the most alive?
Was it when I was feeling sorry for myself
or when I was helping someone?*

Daily Reminder
June 25

Think about it!

HELP

I don't remember exactly when I got hooked on helping people, but I will never forget the rush I got when the person said with tears in their eyes, "Thank you—you have really helped me!" I could obviously see that they meant it! In my life up to then, when people had tears in their eyes, it was not because I had helped them. For the first time in my life I can remember, I felt useful. I was determined I wanted to feel more of that!

Trying is good! Doing is better!

Feeling good because I share love with someone may be selfish, but that is the kind of selfish I want to be!

Daily Reminder
June 26

Think about it!

Have you ever stopped to look at the amount of money, time, energy, and tears one addict costs society in one day? It costs energy and tears from people who care about us and money and time from our legal system. Lawyers are not cheap. Judges who have to listen to our lies are not cheap! Police risking their lives to get us off the street so innocent people don't get harmed are not cheap! The sad thing is, we think society owes us!

EXPENSE

Trying is good! Doing is better!

The longer we use, the more negative and hateful we become! Look back to where you started and puke!

Daily Reminder
June 27

Think about it!

Statistics say that one in ten people are or will become addicts! That is 10 percent of our population! Ten percent of our population are taking instead of giving! Ten percent are ripping the guts out of their **LEGAL** families and our country! The solution we hear is to legalize drugs so there will be less crime! Where do addicts get their money for drugs? Are all addicts hardworking, honest people, or are there some who want to get their money for no work? How is legalizing drugs going to change that?

Trying is good! Doing is better!

What strength will we make the legalized drug? What age limit? I'm twelve, and I want dope! What about me?

Norm Sharkey

**Daily Reminder
June 28**

Think about it!

So we legalize drugs! I just spent my rent money and family's food money on drugs that the government says are now legal to buy at a store! Does the fact drugs are legal make my family feel any more secure tonight than they did when drugs weren't legal? Is their fear of having nowhere to live any different? How about the hunger? Not as bad? The age limit for cigarettes doesn't seem to stop kids from smoking! Why would drugs be different?

INSANITY

Trying is good! Doing is better!

The pain, fear, and hunger our families feel don't go away just because some government legalizes drugs!

Sanity 365

**Daily Reminder
June 29**

Think about it!

What would this world be like if there were no drugs to use as an escape? Would there be as much violence, bank robberies, killings, car wrecks, fraud, bankruptcy, overdoses, child abuse, neglect, or arson? Would we need as many police, courts, lawyers, and judges? Would some of our political decisions make more sense? Would there be a need for food banks in countries that have so much? Looks like we will never find out, doesn't it?

DREAM ON

Trying is good! Doing is better!

My life today does not involve any of the above! I am so grateful to be able to say that I am not perfect, but I sure am better!

185

Norm Sharkey

Daily Reminder
June 30

Think about it!

Alcohol is a legal drug! Are the families of all the alcoholics happy, contented people tonight? Do they sleep better knowing that the alcoholic in their family who will be staggering in and terrorizing them is drinking a legal substance? Perhaps he or she just smashed up the family car and killed a few people! The substance in the alcoholic's body was legal, though, so it's okay! I sound a little ridiculous, don't I? The point I'm trying to make is that we can't control the results of legal drugs, such as alcohol, and we want to legalize some additional drugs!

NO PROBLEM

Trying is good! Doing is better!

There has to be a better solution!
More drugs for all are not the answer! Is it?

186

July

Daily Reminder
July 1

Think about it!

I am assuming the people who are still reading this book are serious about staying clean! I am very fortunate that since I got serious on June 6, 1971, I have not had any kind of compulsion to use drugs. I asked God, as I understand God, to help me and have not had to use! I believe if I had been trying to stay clean without God's help, I would quite likely have returned to dope! God did for me what I thought was impossible!

HELP

Trying is good! Doing is better!

Up until that day, I had no relationship with God, so it is possible for anyone to develop a relationship for sure!

187

Norm Sharkey

Daily Reminder
July 2

Think about it!

At one time in my life, I moved into a small apartment my mom had rented for herself. We needed another bed, so she arranged for a loan from a finance company and told them I would pick it up. The loan was cash, so I had no trouble converting it into drugs. I arrived home very late that night with a newspaper, no money, and no bed. My mother said, "You are just like your father," and slowly shuffled away with tears in her eyes. I'm so proud to be able to tell you this story. Not!

REGRET

Trying is good! Doing is better!

This is just one of many, many such things I selfishly did to people who loved me. How about you? Got some stories?

Daily Reminder
July 3

Think about it!

I used to say that when I found God, such and such happened. What I mean by that is when I came to the point where I was completely desperate, with my back to the wall, as they say, I had to call for help from someone. No one was around, so I asked God to save my miserable life! As the days went by and I was still clean and reasonably happy and grateful, my belief in God gradually got stronger and stronger! It's called faith!

BELIEVE

Happy birthday, Tracey!
Trying is good! Doing is better!

*No one is trying to lay a big religious trip on you.
If you are having trouble staying clean,
God is worth checking out!*

Daily Reminder
July 4

Think about it!

My understanding today of God is very simple! When I love myself and other people, I have a good connection with God! When I don't love myself and others, I push myself away from God! That's how I see it! As a great man called Jesus said, "Love God, love your neighbor, love yourself." If you do that, He said you are doing it all! That seems very simple, and it is! The question is how do I love God, my neighbor, and myself?

LOVE

Trying is good! Doing is better!

In my case, loving me was the most difficult part of the three! I was not a nice person. How about you?

Sanity 365

Daily Reminder
July 5

Think about it!

Drugs make the problems we already have worse! Our problem is living! We can often hide our problems with life until we add drugs to them. Then our problems become obvious to the world. Drugs give us the artificial guts to come out of our shells, and suddenly the world can see the maniacs we are. We, however, are conned by drugs into thinking that everything is fine. Our world of fantasy seems very real to us! The world is a mess, not us.

HIDING

Trying is good! Doing is better!

How is it that we can see that someone else is a mess but we can't see we are too? I'm okay; you're not okay!

Daily Reminder
July 6

Think about it!

I have talked many times about honesty with others and myself! To love myself, I had to be honest about myself with at least one other human! Being honest with God was not a problem, because God has observed me since I was born or maybe even before. Being honest with me was somewhat harder. To be completely honest with another person was the toughest of all! Ego gets in the way. How much should I be honest about?

HONEST?

Trying is good! Doing is better!

If I am honest a little, I will get some freedom. If I am totally honest, I will get total freedom! What do I want?

Daily Reminder
July 7

Think about it!

I fought the idea of revealing my secrets to another person for four years! I had no lasting, contented clean time during those four years. I stayed clean off and on during that time, but I would eventually go back to using. When I got serious about being clean, I knew what I had to do!

OPEN

I am not saying that talking openly about me is easy, but what a relief it was when I was done! I discovered I wasn't any worse or better than any other addicts!

Trying is good! Doing is better!

If you are serious about having a contented, clean future, get serious about the above!

Daily Reminder
July 8

Think about it!

Have you ever stopped to look at the path of destruction you have left behind you during your days of having fun? You destroyed or tried to destroy anyone or anything that got in your way! Loved ones hung on to us, crying and begging us not to go out and use, and we still went! After we got our fix, we would sneak back into the house or apartment and rip off anything we could convert to drugs. Beautiful picture, isn't it? Want to repeat it?

PAIN

Trying is good! Doing is better!

How can we look at our past and still think that drugs are not a problem? How many more people do we have to destroy before it is a problem?

Daily Reminder
July 9

Think about it!

Many times in my life I have asked, "If there is a God who really loves us all, why are there such things as war, earthquakes, famine, etc.?" The answer: I don't know! Sometimes I do think God gets blamed for things that are the fault of humans rather than God!

LOVE

I believe in an afterlife, so if I make it to heaven, I'm assuming God will answer questions like that for me! In the meantime, all I can do is continue to love people!

Happy birthday, Joey!
Trying is good! Doing is better!

*My job is to love people, and so is yours!
Leave the rest of the headaches to God!*

Daily Reminder
July 10

Think about it!

Over the years, I have discovered that I stopped living when I stopped loving! Usually I stopped loving myself first, then other people. When that happened, I just existed; I wasn't living! If I stay in this condition very long, I am setting myself up to get stoned! As I have mentioned several times in this book, I am a selfish person who wants to feel good! For that reason, I will change what is causing the hate and I will get back to loving. I know that using dope will not do the job anymore!

LOVE

Trying is good! Doing is better!

Each day I am clean gives me a chance to understand that the greatest thing in life is to love and be loved!

Sanity 365

Daily Reminder
July 11

Think about it!

The drug culture is a selfish one! The purpose of using drugs is so I can feel better, no matter who else gets hurt. Greed and selfishness are at the center of drug use. Little innocent kids go to school and to bed hungry! They live in an environment of fear and hate. They are left in front of the TV set for hours. They are sexually abused by addicted friends of their parents. Sounds like a beautiful way to learn about life, doesn't it?

DENIAL

Trying is good! Doing is better!

We tell ourselves that we are not hurting anyone but ourselves! How can we honestly believe that? Are we that badly screwed up?

Norm Sharkey

Daily Reminder
July 12

Think about it!

For years, my whole life was built around the "poor me" attitude! My problems were always someone else's fault. If the world would get off my back, I'd be fine.

TODAY

The world was not on my back; it was the drug monkey, and what a load! When I got clean, I had a mountain of problems to deal with, but one day at a time, I began to put my life back together! You can do the same if you just deal with today—not tomorrow, just today.

Trying is good! Doing is better!

If I can't find an answer today, maybe I can tomorrow. As long as I honestly have tried today, there should be no guilt or depression!

Daily Reminder
July 13

Think about it!

Let's see—what excuse can I use today so I can feel depressed? I have many in my files! They seem to be so easy to activate. Drugs gave me a never-ending list. I have many excuses to be depressed but no reasons! I know I have one purpose in this life, and that is to love! Everything else is just window dressing! I can't be responsible for everyone else's actions or motives! All I can do is show love! That's all she wrote!

EXCUSES

Trying is good! Doing is better!

You may not love me, but you can't stop me from loving you! You find that even more frustrating?

Norm Sharkey

Daily Reminder
July 14

Think about it!

Sometimes we think we will live to be two hundred years old! We tell ourselves we have plenty of time to do something with our lives! We were out getting some money for more dope and stuck a knife in someone's belly! Talk about life—that's what we get! Now we will have plenty of time to think about what to do with our lives! The only problem is the opportunities are limited, and so is your travel space!

TIME

Trying is good! Doing is better!

Procrastination is a sin; it causes endless sorrow. We really must stop doing it—in fact, we'll start tomorrow!

200

Daily Reminder
July 15

Think about it!

I don't know why I didn't understand for so many years that to feel good, I have to try and help someone else feel good! That has become a very normal way for me to think today! I have no reason to feel sorry for myself anymore. Everything that has happened in my life, while both stoned and clean, has had a purpose! The purpose is to build gratitude and love! I don't think one exists without the other!

HELP

Trying is good! Doing is better!

As long as God does the thinking and I do the writing, we end up with something on paper worth reading!

Norm Sharkey

**Daily Reminder
July 16**

Think about it!

This is just my miserable opinion, but from experience, I have found that love hurts when it is the wrong kind of love! You may ask how there can be a wrong kind of love. What I call a wrong kind is not really love! It is **SELFISH** an imitation that looks like love but is not! It is taking someone hostage! You are my property and no one else's! I can't live without you, and I don't want anyone else to be with you except me! This is only about me and what I want!

Trying is good! Doing is better!

Unless the other person's wishes and needs are considered, I can't really say I love him or her!

Daily Reminder
July 17

Think about it!

God is still up there laughing! When I was about four years old, I was mad at my brother and tried to throw a brick at him, but instead, I dropped it on my own foot! All through my life, as I tried to get even with someone, I usually dropped the brick on my own foot! How about you? Have you found that payback worked out in your life? The world is in a state of continuous payback, and everyone has lost track of why!

PAYBACK

Trying is good! Doing is better!

We are all full of crap, so why do we think we should pay someone back? Have we never crossed someone, never?

Daily Reminder
July 18

Think about it!

Getting even! What a hateful game! We always seem to feel that if we get even with someone, we will have done something that is very normal in this life. Perhaps what the other person did to us in his or her mind was also very normal. You think the other person is a goof, and the other person thinks you are a goof! So we have two goofs doing what they both think is normal. As we have discovered, getting even under these conditions is usually far from normal! An eye for an eye always ends up with no one being able to see!

CONFUSED

Trying is good! Doing is better!

What I should be looking at is what I did to the person in the first place that caused him or her to do whatever it was he or she did to me! As a result, I could have a chance to change some serious problems in my character!

Sanity 365

Daily Reminder
July 19

Think about it!

For any of us who hit roadblocks every so often, how do we usually get around them? Speaking for myself, I usually kept trying to stagger forward, even when I didn't know what I was doing! More often than not, I made the situation worse instead of better. I may have taken a breather for a few minutes and then plunged forward again! Each time, as I continued to make things worse, I would over and over again tell myself what a stupid idiot I was! Even though I knew I needed help with this project, my ego told me that if I asked for help, I would look even more stupid!

REACH OUT

Trying is good! Doing is better!

Sometimes I believe that even God wants us to ask a human for help! I know when I do ask people, it brings me back down to earth, where I need to live with the rest of you!

Daily Reminder
July 20

Think about it!

I used to think, Why me? Why me? Poor me! Now when I think like that, I am thinking, Why have I been so fortunate to survive all the insanity of addiction?

BELIEVE

Over the years, I have been given such a fantastic, miraculous, and bountiful opportunity to make something of my life! I have been clean since June 6, 1971, continuously, and I believe I have accomplished quite a few worthwhile things! I could have, as I see it today, done an awful lot more! I can only say that if God gives me the time and the health, I will!

Trying is good! Doing is better!

I have found that I usually turn to Him when I am completely lost. It's a thing I seem to repeat over and over—running around in circles, banging my head against the wall! It is a good thing for me that God is so patient or I'm not sure how I would end up most days!

Daily Reminder
July 21

Think about it!

Many times between 1967 and 1971, I thought I was ready to do the changing I needed to stay clean happily! That was about as much as I did, though. I just thought about changing! The more I thought about it, the more convinced I became that I couldn't or didn't think I had to! I would see other people who appeared to be doing okay without changing, so why should I? In time, I went back to using! Change or die!

GET REAL

Trying is good! Doing is better!

For years, drugs and my druggie friends told me I was okay—just misunderstood! If I was okay all the time, why did I need drugs to get by?

**Daily Reminder
July 22**

Think about it!

I was very selfish as a child and even more selfish as a teenager using drugs! Every decision I made was about whether or not I would feel good! Many people who had been my friends before drugs either got pushed aside or walked away. My parents, in my mind, were not my friends; they were just people I put up with! My home was just a place to flop when I had nowhere worthwhile to go. Nice attitude, eh?

ME

Trying is good! Doing is better!

Drug addiction is the selfish disease! It was all about me feeling good! No consideration was given to other people's feelings or their bank accounts! I had to be high!

Daily Reminder
July 23

Think about it!

ESCAPE

I don't deserve what I've gotten, but I'm glad I didn't get what I deserve! The number of times I should've died when I was using is more than I care to remember! As my uncle once said, "You could fall in an outhouse and come out smelling like a rose." We all had plenty of luck on our side when we were stoned. Was it all just luck? Is there a reason why we have survived up until now? Many haven't! Why us?

Trying is good! Doing is better!

In time we come to believe that somebody up there likes us! It's a good thing, because not too many down here did! That does change, thank God!

Norm Sharkey

Daily Reminder
July 24

Think about it!

Selfishness! There is the "addiction type" of selfishness, and the "recovery type" of selfishness. Addiction selfishness says, "I will get stoned no matter who it may affect!" Recovery selfishness says, "I must stay clean straight for me and also for everyone involved in my new life!" If someone says that you have to be selfish about staying clean, it is the recovery selfishness they are talking about! Sometimes in my recovery I have fallen back into the addiction selfishness without getting stoned, and people have turned away from me!

ME! ME! ME!

Trying is good! Doing is better!

The question: will someone get hurt if I use?
Answer: yes! The question: will someone get hurt if I change and stay clean? Answer: no!

**Daily Reminder
July 25**

Think about it!

If it feels good, do it! That was the cry of the '60s generation! When I got stoned, I found that deciding if it felt good was an easy to justify using! My conscience was replaced by drugs, so everything felt good. **SELFISH** Doing whatever came into my head was good! Whether or not people would be affected never entered into the thought process! It was just about me and if it felt good! I go through a different thinking process when I am clean. A bit more reality is involved in the thinking!

Trying is good! Doing is better!

Even when my guts tell me no, I have at times done what I wanted to do anyway. I discovered very quickly that if someone got hurt as a result, I had to make things right with them or risk getting stoned!

Norm Sharkey

**Daily Reminder
July 26**

Think about it!

Have you ever wondered what your purpose is in this life? Surely at times you have asked what it is all about. Some people are born blind, deaf, disabled, mute, or with diseases that take away their lives very early. A great percentage of addicts are born healthy and within years, try as hard as they can to disable themselves with drugs! Somewhere along the way, we have to take a good look around us. Why me?

SURVIVED

Trying is good! Doing is better!

What have I done to deserve my health, love from friends and family, and opportunity to live a good life and help others? What?

Daily Reminder
July 27

Think about it!

So now you're clean! What are you going to do or try to do with your life? Is it possible to turn all the dreams that were just dreams into reality? No one is more determined than addicts to prove to the world that we can accomplish all sorts of wild things! Well? When do we get started? Will we just continue talking about what we can do and then get stoned again? Or will we actually draw up a plan and get on with it?

TALK?

Trying is good! Doing is better!

Failing at something, providing you stay clean, is not the end of the world! Doing nothing is what will cause you to go backward!

Norm Sharkey

Daily Reminder
July 28

Think about it!

One thing I have discovered over the years is that addicts are very talented people! Motivation seems to be our biggest problem. Sticking with something and seeing it to a successful finish is also a problem.

DO IT!

Every time we give up on something that we and others have felt was good, we seem to lose a little more confidence in our own ability. When using, we lacked confidence unless we were stoned! Don't quit on your project or yourself! You can do it!

Trying is good! Doing is better!

If your real friends are telling you that you can succeed, believe them! How long did you believe in drugs, which were not real!

Daily Reminder
July 29

Think about it!

NOWHERE MAN

Many times in my life, I said I wanted to get clean and I thought I meant it! I wish I could count the number of times I was sure I would get clean and went back to using. I still thought I could beat the game. I had not changed my thinking, habits, or personality. I had just stopped using. You can only stay clean so long that way. The addiction animal is alive and well, ready to get active when it sees no one on guard!

Trying is good! Doing is better!

Changing who we are and hanging out with winners is important if we want to stay clean!

Daily Reminder
July 30

Think about it!

POWER

Amazing things happen when I get out of the way and let God do the leading! I may do some of the legwork, but God connects the dots! Even with this book, I do the writing, but God does the thinking! If you are struggling and trying to get or stay clean, maybe it is time to get serious about involving Him in your efforts! Addiction is something human willpower alone cannot overcome! God definitely did and does supply the power I need!

Trying is good! Doing is better!

Remember, folks; it's the God of your understanding, not mine or religion's. You and God and people! Don't get all crazy now—just do it! It will work!

Daily Reminder
July 31

Think about it!

I sometimes worry that the mention of God in these pages will turn people away. In my own case, it didn't, because I had nowhere else to turn! I had tried every other approach with no success. So I finally decided to give Him a chance! God is love, and I sure needed a bunch of that! When I see love in someone's eyes or in their actions, I see God! Try to look at it that way!

OPEN MIND

Trying is good! Doing is better!

I can do little! We can do much! Many people will die today because of drugs. If we are not one of them, let's get busy and see who we can help!

August

Daily Reminder
August 1

Think about it!

ACTION

I need help, and I'm ready to do whatever I need to do to get clean and stay clean! You are? Yes! Do you have any dope on you? Yes! Flush it down the toilet! Okay, now what? Now we get started on a new life! You have any charges? Yes! Are you ready to do time, if you have to? Yes! Will you stay clean in jail? Yes! If you mean all that, we can do business! The next day, this person is stoned!

Trying is good! Doing is better!

We often have good intentions. That is not enough!
We need good intentions and solid actions
if we are to succeed!

Norm Sharkey

Daily Reminder
August 2

Think about it!

I think sometimes we feel that if we ask God into our lives, we will instantly have to become perfect! If that was the case, I would have died stoned many years ago! Just as a good friend doesn't want to see me do things to hurt others or myself, God simply tries to get my attention through my conscience! I believe God is that little voice that says, "I don't think that would be a smart thing to do!" It's then my decision.

FRIEND

Trying is good! Doing is better!

Even when I go ahead and do something dumb, just like a good friend, He is still ready to love and help me! Beat it if you can!

220

Sanity 365

**Daily Reminder
August 3**

Think about it!

Sometimes we only need a small spark to get us burning again! Seeing someone we haven't seen for years and seeing how well they look can be the inspiration we need to get back on track! "If they can do it, I can do it," is often the message we get! That is why if we are clean today. You and I have an obligation to stay that way as an example for people who are not as fortunate! It's the grace of God! Remember?

EXAMPLE

Trying is good! Doing is better!

Because we are clean doesn't mean we are better than someone who is not! It simply means we are in a much better position to be able to change who we are!

Daily Reminder
August 4

Think about it!

I am not a handyman! Therefore, I use this excuse to not try certain projects. When I do try something and screw it up, it confirms in my mind I shouldn't even have tried! Sometimes, though, things do fall into place, and I walk around like I just built the Empire State Building. Everything we try may not bring the results we are hoping for, but we can't stop trying. If your intentions are pure, the results will look after them! You can plan the plan, but you can't plan the results!

EXTREMES

Trying is good! Doing is better!

We need to forgive even more than we need forgiveness. Forgive others so they can forgive others and on and on and on!

Daily Reminder
August 5

Think about it!

For many years I walked around trying to give the world the impression that I was okay! Inside, I was dying! Today, what you see is what you get! If I look okay, I am okay! If I don't, I'm not! This way I can get help, because people can see I need it if I am messed up! No camouflage! What I am saying, folks, is that if you are hurting, ask for help! Perhaps you will help someone else just by talking about yourself!

OPEN

Trying is good! Doing is better!

We have no idea what we can do until we get out and get at it! We are not hopeless, useless people! Come on, let's go!

Norm Sharkey

Daily Reminder
August 6

Think about it!

LIAR, LIAR

Anything of importance I wanted to do is impossible the moment I pick up some dope. The doing stops, and the excuses get bigger! "I can't do this because everyone is against me!" Ta–da–ta–da–ta–da! Drugs make instant liars out of us! I couldn't believe I was able to think up some of the lies I told! Drugs helped me become an expert liar! I am sure today there are people who still think I am a liar, but there's nothing I can do about that except show them otherwise!

Trying is good! Doing is better!

'No one expects us to conquer the world! Most people know we can't! They just want to see us clean. Is that good enough for you?

Daily Reminder
August 7

Think about it!

Givers are winners! Takers are losers! Look at twenty people you know, both clean and stoned! The people who try to make someone else's life happier I am sure are much happier than the people who try to rip them off! Givers may appear to be "suckers" to some people, but at the end of the day, look who is still standing on their feet with smiles on their faces! Takers cannot feel better at the end of the day because they have done nothing but take from people!

GIVER

Trying is good! Doing is better!

The emptiness you feel will disappear from you as you help others try to be winners! Give someone some of your time. You may make a friend for life!

Norm Sharkey

Daily Reminder
August 8

Think about it!

I met a man the other day I hadn't seen for many years. At one point in his life, he was clean for a long period of time! He told me he had started to smoke a little pot, and before he knew it, he was doing crack! People say pot will not lead to harder drugs! Tell him that! I plan to see him again. I believe he wants help, and if he does, I will do what I can to help him!

PROGRESSIVE

Trying is good! Doing is better!

Our streets are filled with crime and the walking dead! What can I do today? What can you do today? What can we do today?

Daily Reminder
August 9

Think about it!

Today is the most important day of your life and my life! What we are able to do today will determine tomorrow, next week, next month, and next year! It all starts with today! A positive day today leads to the opportunity for a positive day tomorrow! Sounds rather simple, but just living and loving today are a lot more difficult than they sound! When I do live completely within this day, I have one of the most relaxing, rewarding days in my life! Give it a go!

NOW

Trying is good! Doing is better!

Leave tomorrow for tomorrow! If you're like I was in my first few days clean, your mind is racing one thousand miles an hour! Just today, guys! Just today!

Norm Sharkey

Daily Reminder
August 10

Think about it!

Happiness comes as a result of a well-lived life! The thoughts I have and put into action will determine my happiness today! I don't depend on others to make me happy; I have the ability to do that for myself. Besides that, if I make other people happy, I will in turn increase my own happiness. It works exactly the same way if I put people on a bummer! We can't all be comedians, but we can add a spark to someone's life every day! It will come back to us!

HAPPY

Trying is good! Doing is better!

Did you hear about the Australian who bought a new boomerang and went crazy trying to throw the old one away?

Daily Reminder
August 11

Think about it!

If you help someone up the hill, you're that much closer to the top yourself! Together, we can do what one can't! On my own, I can stay clean, but not as happily as I can if I'm sharing with others! A room with one clean person does not attract people the same way a room full of clean, happy people does! Sure, not everyone in the room is happy, but what they see and feel from the ones who are happy is something they know they want! Are they ready to work for it? That's the big question!

US

Trying is good! Doing is better!

Our responsibility to others is also our responsibility to ourselves. We must change if we want to remain clean and happy and show others how to do the same!

Daily Reminder
August 12

Think about it!

It is sometimes easy to forget the amount of time and help people showered on me when I decided I was serious about staying clean! People gave up time with their families to spend with me! They spent hours on the telephone, tying their lines up that perhaps were also business lines! They listened to my complaints, my needs, and my wants, and my hatred of the world was not a positive experience for them! They never once closed their doors or hung up on me! I owe! I owe! I owe! It's off to work I go!

I OWE

Trying is good! Doing is better!

If people were in a burning house, would we just leave them there to die? There are people dying because of drugs today! What is our action plan? Nothing?

Daily Reminder
August 13

Think about it!

CHOICES

There are many different methods we can use to stay clean! Some methods work well for some people; other methods work well with others. If the method you have been offered by whoever does not appeal to you, don't use it as an excuse to get stoned. Just look for a different method! There is no sense killing yourself because someone offered you apples and you wanted oranges! Go and find some oranges, right? I'll get even with them; I'll kill myself. This is not the solution.

Trying is good! Doing is better!

It makes sense to me that if I am clean and happy, I probably will not trade it for stoned and happy unless my clean and happy is phony!

Norm Sharkey

Daily Reminder
August 14

Think about it!

You may ask, "What can I do?" The world is full of miracle workers who at one time asked the same question. You don't have to save the world. Just start with one person—yourself! We are all so ready to change other people, but we sometimes forget about ourselves! I can only help you if I, at the same time, help me! You do not want a big speech; you want to hear what I did to find a way out of the insanity!

HELP

Trying is good! Doing is better!

Help me to help you! When people allow me to help them, I will suddenly become alive. God deserves the credit, because all my life I was too selfish to help anyone else! He is power and love!

Sanity 365

***Daily Reminder*
August 15**

Think about it!

When we are given the privilege of helping people (and it is a privilege), we often get started with a lot of enthusiasm and positive energy! We are going to get this person clean! Right! Perhaps our friends begin to change their minds when they see how much work they have to do! Usually then we begin to get critical of them and begin demanding, "You better!" The more we do that, the more they back off! Eventually there is a shouting match, and the person is using again! We can't get anyone clean! We can help, that's all!

LOVE

Trying is good! Doing is better!

You can lead a horse to water, but you can't make him drink! Leave the water there. They may get thirsty later! Who knows when they are ready? Do you? Love! Remember?

Norm Sharkey

**Daily Reminder
August 16**

Think about it!

We mentioned a Good, Orderly Direction earlier on in this book. We are not trying to sell you on any religion or faith. We have discovered over the years that the people who do hook up with God, as they understand God, seem to survive the temptation to use again better than the people who do not establish a spiritual connection. This, however, is entirely up to each person! If you wish to leave God out of the picture, then that is your business!

DECISION

Trying is good! Doing is better!

I can be as happy or as bummed out as I want to be today! It is my life, and it is I who will decide! I'm very selfish, so I think I will be happy—without drugs, too!

Sanity 365

Daily Reminder
August 17

Think about it!

Perhaps the person I'm trying to help does not see all the good qualities in me I think I have! Perhaps I need to start looking a little closer at myself to see if I'm doing as well as I think I am! Sometimes when my life ticks along like a clock, I don't see the iceberg under the water continually looking at me to patch up any leaks will ensure my boat doesn't sink! God is the glue!

CHECKING

Trying is good! Doing is better!

We're all here because we're not all there! Maybe you are, but I'm not, and I see that more and more every day.

Norm Sharkey

**Daily Reminder
August 18**

Think about it!

Here I go on value one of my journey! I admitted I was powerless over any kind of drugs and my life had become a mess! I can also be a mess when I'm clean. But add dope, and it's a complete disaster!

GOOD TIMES?

Anytime I think life is difficult now, I only need to look at what it was then! If I don't see any difference, I'm in big trouble! I will be getting ready to use again!

Trying is good! Doing is better!

We may look back on our using days and say, "I had some good times!" Perhaps I did, but for how long and at whose expense? Was it good times that made you think you should get clean, really?

Daily Reminder
August 19

Think about it!

I've never seen a grateful addict get stoned! If we are clean and aren't grateful, there is something wrong with the program we are doing. We have lost sight of how things used to be! We have begun to feel smug and righteous. We may even say, "I will never use again." Our survival depends on our actions today! If you are grateful, you may say, "Today, I feel like I will never use again." Then back up the words with action!

ACTION

Trying is good! Doing is better!

There are no bad days if you are clean! Some days are just better than others! Look at your worst clean day. Look at your worst day stoned!

Norm Sharkey

Daily Reminder
August 20

Think about it!

DIFFERENCES

If I am not clean happy, I will try being stoned happy! There are only two ways to happiness for me! Sometimes stoned happy seems to be the easiest way, but is it? No, otherwise why would I look for clean happy? Clean happy requires hard work and honesty! Stoned happy also requires hard work and plenty of lies! Clean happy requires me to become a better, honest, loving human being. Stoned happy requires me to become more of a sneak, liar, and thief! I'll take clean happy, thank you!

Trying is good! Doing is better!

If we are clean for a while, why should there be any confusion over how we should remain? When problems arise and we don't deal with them, then that is when the confusion begins!

Sanity 365

Daily Reminder
August 21

Think about it!

ANIMAL

I am clean for awhile—enjoying all the benefits that go with being clean, such as being able to sleep, getting rid of paranoia, feeling love and respect from family and friends, going back to school or work, and feeling healthy, to name a few! I now have a few dollars in the bank, a car, and a decent place to live and slowly start to forget how bad things were when I was using! How could I, you say? How could I possibly forget? The animal is just waiting for me to get cocky, and then it will hit me harder than ever!

Happy birthday, Judy!
Trying is good! Doing is better!

My life was a mess! If I really believe that, I will get down to working on the rest of the values to recovery!

Daily Reminder
August 22

Think about it!

COMPARING

Gratitude usually fills us when we see some poor addict exactly where we used to be! We are not grateful because they are screwed up but grateful because we are not, at that particular time. If we stop trying to change, we can be right back there too! The animal is alive and well, ready to take you down if you're not on guard! We can never think we are better than someone else—just better off! As long as you stay clean, you may be able to help that person find freedom!

Trying is good! Doing is better!

The reason why we're all the same is because we all thought we were different!

Sanity 365

Daily Reminder
August 23

Think about it!

Value two: Through being open and honest with fellow addicts, we came to know a power we could depend on called God! Honesty brings freedom! Honesty brings hope! Honesty brings love! Honesty connects us to God as we begin to understand God! We stay open and honest with fellow addicts and then open and honest with everyone! You may need to bounce some things off other addicts first before you go to your family with them! Through discussing things with other addicts who have done this value, you will understand the importance of honesty!

HONEST

Trying is good! Doing is better!

This is the value; if you do it thoroughly, that will give you the feeling that there is a power you can call on to get you through the tough times!

Daily Reminder
August 24

Think about it!

You may say, "I did value two, but I still don't feel that close to God or any other power!" You just don't do the value like you are writing an exam in school! It is something you have to do every day! If I don't

DO IT

involve all six values in my day, I probably will not have this clean, happy day that I am looking for! Most of us are great in the fifty-yard dash but not worth a damn in the hundred-yard dash! Keep going!

Trying is good! Doing is better!

In many competitions, we stubbornly refused to quit! Why is it when our life is involved, we are so ready to give up?

Daily Reminder
August 25

Think about it!

When we are tied to a railroad track and the train is ten feet away, that's usually when we decide it's time to get clean! That's when we get religion! I'll do this, I'll do that, just stop the train. The train stops, so we change our minds. Things aren't so bad. I only lost one leg. I can still hustle with one leg! Cheer up, guys, things could get worse, and they do! Soon we'll have no legs! No arms! Who cares! Not you, obviously!

I'M OKAY

Trying is good! Doing is better!

We wonder why non-addicts look at us a little strangely! They have heard our promises for years now. Nothing changes!

Norm Sharkey

Daily Reminder
August 26

Think about it!

I guess the reason I had so much difficulty dealing with problems when I got clean was because in the stoner's world, we had so many problems on the go at any one time that we didn't even bother to deal with them; we just stayed high! Also, we usually left other people to deal with our problems! Only the really serious people will be prepared to deal with problems clean and move on with life! I hope this does not offend anyone, but like me, until you have reached the garbage dump and have nowhere to go but a smellier garbage dump, dealing with problems will not be something you will look forward to! Nobody looks forward to dealing with problems, but the people who do will get stronger as each day goes by!

REMEMBER

Trying is good! Doing is better!

I am very grateful today that I can still remember my last day on the street like it was yesterday! I have no problem remembering when! I strongly believe that as long as I can feel in my guts what it was like, moving forward through any problems will seem like child's play! I have had a terrific number of wonderful days since I've been clean! I also know there are many more to come!

Daily Reminder
August 27

Think about it!

One thing for sure is that if you hang in, talk about your problems, and get the help you need to deal with them, things will get better! Guaranteed! I say again, guaranteed! I wandered around my friend's garage on my first day clean like a lunatic! I couldn't sit still for a moment! I must have walked ten thousand miles that afternoon! Greg was working on cars and still had the time to talk with me and try to slow me down! There is one thing I remember him saying, and I hope that repeating it will help someone to get through this day clean! He said he wished he could put me into next year so I could experience how good being clean that long would feel! Thanks to Greg and God, as I understand God, I made it through that day and many, many more after that! Stay with us! It's worth it!

SICK

Trying is good! Doing is better!

You may be thinking that it's easy for me to say, "Stay with us," but I don't feel as bad as you do! I have no way of knowing whether you feel worse than I did on that last day. I can only tell you that I would have needed a bigger body and a bigger head to have felt any sicker on that day! Let's leave it at that!

Daily Reminder
August 28

Think about it!

Everyone has problems. That was something I was not aware of when I first got clean. The first few days or weeks, everything seemed to go my way! Then, little by little, I started to encounter some small negatives! "When will these problems ever end?" I would ask. I thought life was supposed to be easy when you put away the drugs! I was such a baby! All the years I did drugs, I was not aware that normal people in some cases have more problems than I could ever imagine! In my using days, my solution to problems was stoning them away and not solving them! Therefore, it took a considerable amount of time to develop the skills needed to try and solve any problems that came along!

POOR ME!

Trying is good! Doing is better!

Talking to other people and understanding that problems are a normal part of life are and were very important for me! I thank God that I have lived long enough in this great way of life to finally see that if I don't quit, I can get through any problem! This is what most addicts who successfully stay clean have come to realize!

Sanity 365

Daily Reminder
August 29

Think about it!

Value three: With the help of God and our friends, we took an honest look at ourselves and became willing to change the things that were keeping us high! Just exactly what would these things be? Let's see! How about things like hate, dishonesty, jealousy, selfishness, poor me, and gossip, just for starters! These cancers can separate me from God and real people! With this sort of garbage active in my life, it is impossible for me to love myself, let alone anyone else.

OH! NO!

Trying is good! Doing is better!

We can't do all of this at once, but we have to be ready to start with at least one today! Try going all day without telling a lie!

Daily Reminder
August 30

Think about it!

How did you do with honesty yesterday? If you had success, I'm sure you slept well and got up with more energy today! If you don't stay on guard, you'll find yourself falling back into the "it wasn't me" trips!

HONESTY

I remember once when I was trying to develop honesty habits, I stopped myself in the middle of the story and said, "Sorry. What I was just telling you was a lie!" That, believe me, was a little hard on the ego! As a result, I worked harder on honesty so I wouldn't have to go through that again!

Trying is good! Doing is better!

You may say, "Why do I have to be so honest?" If you're not honest, why do you expect me or anyone else in the world to be honest with you? Maybe everyone in the world is lying! No?

Daily Reminder
August 31

Think about it!

From July 1967 until June 1971, I was in and out of recovery five times. I did very little about changing my living habits. I thought all I had to do was stop using drugs! The person I was in June 1971 was the same person I was in July 1967. I thank God that I lived long enough to see that I had to change me if I wanted success in living clean! Besides, I didn't like the person I was, so why wouldn't I want to change? Changing can be another addiction. Try it!

CHANGE

Trying is good! Doing is better!

This clean life is an adventure in living you won't want to miss! Just like a roller coaster! Enjoy!

September

**Daily Reminder
September 1**

Think about it!

Just as we don't get sunshine every day, we also may have a problem or two in our clean life! Why are we so ready to go back to using just because we have a problem on any given day? I have discovered that I create most of my own problems! Even after years of living clean, I neglect to deal with overdue situations, and they become problems! I usually cannot blame anyone but me! If I have a problem, so do millions of other people! Deal with it!

PROBLEMS

Trying is good! Doing is better!

Problem solving is usually not anything mind-boggling! It simply requires us doing and not just thinking about it!

Norm Sharkey

**Daily Reminder
September 2**

Think about it!

I've never had a problem that did not have a solution! I often did not like the solution, but there was always one there! Normally I would not take any action on the solution because it seemed too scary! That is what it was too! It just seemed scary, but when I took action, the fear was a myth! I discovered people are very forgiving and cooperative as long as I am honest with them! The solution—be straightforward and unafraid!

GUTS!

Trying is good! Doing is better!

God, as I understand Him, gives me the guts to do something about problems! Again, as long as I am honest, there is always a suitable solution!

Sanity 365

**Daily Reminder
September 3**

Think about it!

One of the reasons we recommend God to people who are trying to regroup is so they have someone else to blame when things go wrong—just kidding! You will discover, though, that sometimes when you are alone and have an urge to use, if you ask God (as mysterious as God may seem) to take the urge away, if you are serious, it will go! This is the experience of millions of people over the years! They can't all be whacked!

OH, YEAH?

Trying is good! Doing is better!

The people who are serious about staying clean will take this advice. The ones who aren't will have to stub their toes a little longer!

Norm Sharkey

Daily Reminder
September 4

Think about it!

Another reason why I recommend God to people who are serious is that until I got on my knees and desperately asked to live and stay clean, the urge to use was with me quite often! I don't know about you, but in my case, if I had an urge to use, I usually ended up using! God took the craving away! I believe as long as I work at the six values every day, God will look after the drug part! That has been my experience anyway!

TRUST

Trying is good! Doing is better!

If the craving was taken away and then comes back, perhaps more work on the six values is needed! Again, honesty!

Daily Reminder
September 5

Think about it!

CREDIT

It's hard to be humble! It feels so good when some one says, "You deserve a lot of credit for what you have done with your life." I would like to take all the compliments—believe me I would—but I know and you know that I haven't done all that much! All I did was ask God for help so I wouldn't die, and He showed me the recipe to follow as long as I was serious! I simply say, "Thank you for the compliment." If I tell them what I just told you, they will think I am really humble! Get it?

Trying is good! Doing is better!

Here's a good plan to follow if you want to return to drugs! Accept all the credit when things go right and when things go wrong, blame God! The results will follow!

Daily Reminder
September 6

Think about it!

Our journey will be the long way home because we got so lost and disoriented that our recovery will seem like a game of snakes and ladders—moving ahead and falling back.

WINNER!

The urge to say, "To hell with it" will often hit you, but don't give up. We were stubborn when we were using, and we have to be stubborn if we want to win this fight. Have you got what it takes to win this fight? Sure you have! We believe in you! Hang in there!

Trying is good! Doing is better!

The Winners Club is made up of a bunch of people who used to be losers! I'm one of them. I've been clean since June 6, 1971. It will work!

Sanity 365

Daily Reminder
September 7

Think about it!

CHANGE

When I finally put the dope away, I didn't realize there were some serious flaws in my personality that needed to be changed! Just as I was not honest with my using friends, they were not honest with me! We told each other what great humans we were, and we believed it! This attitude was difficult to correct! The people who cared about me slowly were able to get me to see that these flaws were the difference between being able to live happy clean or return to using!

Trying is good! Doing is better!

Let's face some facts, guys! If we needed additives in our life so we could feel happy, there was obviously something missing in our makeup! No? Yes?

Norm Sharkey

Daily Reminder
September 8

Think about it!

You might be wise to ask people who have done value four what the best way may be to approach certain people! These are people who you caused a pile of pain! This is not a car that needs a little tune-up! If they had done to you what you did to them, what would you expect from them? Again, you're just not doing some sort of oral test to pass your drivers exam! This is blood and guts! That's what we took from these people!

CHANGING

Trying is good! Doing is better!

Do value four properly, and you will feel like a new person when you're finished! Don't, and you will probably return to drugs!

Daily Reminder
September 9

Think about it!

Our children have been through an emotional meat grinder while we were using, so you have to understand that they will need some reassuring that the war is over. Depending on their age, they may have done some drug experimenting of their own. They do what they see their parents do!

HUGS

A long period of "rehab" lies ahead. Hopefully it can be done as a family so all can benefit. Now, finally, your responsibility as parents has arrived. You can do it!

Trying is good! Doing is better!

If you missed out on love when you were a kid, don't let your kids miss out! Hug them, and show them you love them!

Daily Reminder
September 10

Think about it!

When we were using, we were like the hamster in the wheel! Nothing changed until we got out of the wheel! How many times when we were spinning around did we see the same scenery? We continued spinning and expected to see something different! We may get a different rush with different drugs, but still, we have the same end result when we come down! Crap! So we tried to stay stoned! Unless we were billionaires, what was the price of staying stoned?

LOST

Trying is good! Doing is better!

Our mind is usually the first thing to check out on us! When it goes, what use is our body?

Daily Reminder
September 11

Think about it!

This is a day many people in the world will never forget! I often wonder if the people involved in this insanity were stoned. I can't believe people who were even close to being in their right minds could have done what they did! I believe that it is the type of hate that drugs can produce! Every addict has had insane thoughts of revenge, but it takes the addition of drugs to give them the guts to put the thoughts into action!

WHACKED!

Trying is good! Doing is better!

To some degree, we all have living problems, but add drugs and it's like adding gasoline to a smoldering fire! Stand back, folks!

Norm Sharkey

Daily Reminder
September 12

Think about it!

SELFISH, LOST

The kids in an addicted family really pay the price for the good times their parents are having. They have sleepless nights because their parents have friends over all night and nothing for breakfast because their parents have crashed or gone out. They are unable to concentrate at school because they're worried about what they will go home to. It's a life of continuous chaos: parents fighting, police being called . . . it never stops! Meanwhile we say, "I'm not hurting anyone but myself." We sure are lost.

Trying is good! Doing is better!

We sure have a huge reconstruction job to do when we do get clean! We have many lives, including our own, to repair. We did the tearing down, so we have to do the building up!

Sanity 365

**Daily Reminder
September 13**

Think about it!

Statistics say one in ten people are addicted to some form of drugs! How is it that 10 percent of the population can cause the other 90 percent to dance to their tune? If this 10 percent were not out of control, would we need such large police forces, medical budgets, prisons, mental institution, fire departments, and social assistance programs? I don't know, something to look at, eh? Will we ever look at it? Probably not, because the 90 percent don't seem to connect the dots!

HELP

Trying is good! Doing is better!

About all I can do today is be sure I don't become one of the 10 percent again! So can you!

Daily Reminder
September 14

Think about it!

Value five: We continued to take a look at ourselves on a daily basis, and when anything bothered us, we talked about it! If we do this value completely every day, we will remain sane enough that we won't see the need for any dope! How can we solve problems when drugs tell us there is no problem? Drugs are like headache pain relievers. Maybe I should see what is causing the headache, huh? Examining me and talking with some else about me just may uncover the pain. Is it worth a try?

CHECKING

Trying is good! Doing is better!

How are you today? I'm fine! That answer comes out very quickly, eh? Is that the real answer or the expected answer?

Daily Reminder
September 15

Think about it!

ESCAPE

We get clean to avoid death and discover so much more! As we look in the rearview mirror at the minefield we have escaped from, we begin to realize how fortunate we were to get out alive! Gratitude takes over from hate and fear. We begin to smile and even laugh, not at someone but at something wholesome and funny! The nightmares we used to have regularly have almost disappeared. Little by little, we are getting healthy in mind and body!

Trying is good! Doing is better!

Religious people talk about being born again. That is how we feel when we get clean. We have been given a second chance!

Norm Sharkey

***Daily Reminder
September 16***

Think about it!

One thing that most of us discover when it comes to dope is that if we don't get our asses kicked very, very, very, hard, we'll go back to using until we do! Not all of us are fortunate enough to survive the kicking.

FIREPROOF?

Many, many, many die or get locked up! We have survived so many times that we always think there's another chance! We're not fireproof, folks! Somewhere along the line, we'll have to pay the price! Then the crying starts!

Happy birthday, Ruth!
Trying is good! Doing is better!

I lived to talk about it! Maybe you won't! You say, "Who cares?" People who love you do! The truth is, you do too!

Daily Reminder
September 17

Think about it!

I'm sure we all know many brilliant people who have checked out or are locked up because of drugs! If they had discovered what life can be like without dope, what would they have contributed to our world?

WHO CARES?

"Who cares?" was also their attitude, but society lost as a result! It seems that the ones with the most talent are the ones who want a free ride! It's not free, though, is it? Do we have to die to discover that?

Trying is good! Doing is better!

Isn't it great to see someone we used to do dope with and see them clean? One less person to go down in flames! One more person who can give instead of take!

Norm Sharkey

Daily Reminder
September 18

Think about it!

Statistics say that each using addict affects sixteen people with his or her actions! If you are clean today, that's sixteen people you're not screwing with—

SOLUTIONS

sixteen people who have had a chance to live a reasonable, normal life today! Some of them are kids who get a restful sleep and won't go to school hungry. Some are parents who don't have to pace the floor all night worrying. Some are employers who won't have to do your work today, bosses who know they will get production from you—and so on!

Trying is good! Doing is better!

When we get clean, it is like a tornado stops in our lives and our loved ones and friends! Keep it that way!

**Daily Reminder
September 19**

Think about it!

We are so lost and unaware of what is happening in the world when we are using! Hundreds of people could die in a disaster of some sort and we would shrug our shoulders and say, "So what?" We overdose, and **PUKE!** the world has to stop! Our families develop sickness because they are worried so much! Who cares, right? I'm okay! Why are they worried about me? If they're that worried, why don't they give me money when I need it? Puke! Puke! Puke! Puke!

Trying is good! Doing is better!

Some countries give an addict one chance to get clean! If you don't take it, then kiss your ass good-bye! Here, we get free needles! What a country, eh?

Norm Sharkey

**Daily Reminder
September 20**

Think about it!

Value six: With God and our friends, we tried to give other addicts what we received and followed these values in our daily living! We say, "Try to give other addicts what we received." We can't give it if they won't take it. The person on the receiving end has to wrap his or her arms around the gift or it will just fall to the floor! This is too precious a gift to be wasted, so we must look for someone else who will grab it.

THE GIFT

Trying is good! Doing is better!

Many people have and will die not knowing what happy clean is all about! Don't be one of them! Start applying the six values to your life right now!

Daily Reminder
September 21

Think about it!

One day, God saw me on my knees in a skid row rooming house and said, "If I don't help this person, he will die stoned." At the same time, I finally got serious about getting clean, so it worked! I do believe when you reach the point where you are serious about getting clean, God will find you! From then on, trying to live the clean life will be much easier than it was the previous day! God knows when you're sincere, and so will the people around you!

GET REAL!

Trying is good! Doing is better!

*Telling you I love you means nothing unless
I show you through my actions.*

Daily Reminder
September 22

Think about it!

Trying to help people find their way is an experience that makes you feel useful for once in your life! Value six is the chance to pay back what people have done for you and me! Once I started trying to help people, I realized how little I knew about helping! As a result, if I didn't want to look like a phony, I had to apply the values to my life so I could tell people what I had done to get well!

WORK

Trying is good! Doing is better!

This is one time when I have to live what I'm talking; otherwise, people will not buy it! No counterfeit bills accepted!

Sanity 365

Daily Reminder
September 23

Think about it!

In many cases, people don't grab the gift right away because they still think they can control things! Perhaps they are getting by—holding down a job, making ends meet, etc. Is that all there is to life? Hanging on until we can retire? Have you ever honestly sat down and calculated how much of your hard-earned money goes to dope? Most people avoid doing that because they are afraid what the figures might be! It could be the difference between owning and renting for the rest of your life.

EXISTING

Trying is good! Doing is better!

Drugs promise a lot and deliver nothing!
When the drugs wear off, the promises go with them!
Why not try something real?

Daily Reminder
September 24

Think about it!

I'm sick and petrified! I can't sit still. I'm having chest pains! I'm going to throw up any minute now! Don't these people know I'll never make it? How long have I been here? Seems like three hours! Fifteen minutes? I need a fix! God, I'm sick! Pass the bucket. What if someone comes in who knows me? How long have I been here? I need a fix! Man, I'm sick! I'll never make it! Pass the bucket!

SICK

Trying is good! Doing is better!

Remember that first day clean! Burn it into your brain so you will never forget! That was and is your first step into freedom! Today I will remember not to forget!

Daily Reminder
September 25

Think about it!

Sitting in the corner of a bar, picking away at the label on the bottle! Washing a few more pills down, trying to figure what it's all about! Where am I going, and when will the insanity stop? Everything inside me feels dead! Where have the years gone? If it weren't for drugs, would I be sitting here? Everyone in this place looks the way I feel! Hopeless! I'm here, doing time! Oh, oh! Time to start smiling; here comes my old buddy Dave!

PRETEND

Trying is good! Doing is better!

Is this you, friend? Tired of hearing people say, "Cheer up"? Laugh in public and die in private. It doesn't have to be this way, you know!

Norm Sharkey

**Daily Reminder
September 26**

Think about it!

There are many addicts who look around and say, "I can't be an addict; otherwise, all my friends are!" That was me for a long time! The truth was that most of my friends were! That is why it is so easy to convince yourself there is no problem! Because you can see now that there is a problem doesn't mean you are evil! It just means that over the years, you have developed dependence. Sex, drugs, and rock and roll, Right? We begin to feel that one without the other two won't produce the expected results!

BUT MONSIEUR!

Trying is good! Doing is better!

Maybe for you, this is a fact! For me, sex and rock and roll work fine! It's a lot healthier and cheaper!

Daily Reminder
September 27

Think about it!

ANSWERS

Sit down with some people who have been clean for a while. Just listen! They know of what they speak—many years of research into life, stoned and clean. Take from them what you need to start building your own life! It does not have to be exactly like theirs. We are not creating clones; we hope to create real, free people. If that's what your hope is, you should succeed, one day at a time! Remember, not everything will work like clockwork, but it will work!

Trying is good! Doing is better!

Each day we meet more and more loving people!
Ask them what they did to get that way!
There are answers, believe me!

Norm Sharkey

**Daily Reminder
September 28**

Think about it!

The clubs and bars are full of happy people! Not! The clubs and bars are full of stoned people trying to be happy! We all want the world to think we are real, together people, so we put on our stage clothes and perform! Stories we heard in some other city become our stories so we can appear a little more exciting! We wish! Then the music stops, the lights go out, and if we're lucky, we end up with someone just as lost as we are!

LOST

Trying is good! Doing is better!

As long as we're with someone, regardless how pathetic, we don't have to think! What a fun life!

Sanity 365

Daily Reminder
September 29

Think about it!

You're addicted! I'm dependant! What's the difference? Who cares? We're both screwed up! You got clean when you still had a job, a car, and a place to live!

COMPARE

Smart move! It sure makes rebuilding an awful lot easier! Perhaps the bills have piled up a bit, but that can be worked out in time, which is something that's on your side now! You will find that you don't mind going to work now! The air will start to smell different; food in the morning will be something to look forward to!

Trying is good! Doing is better!

Gratitude was a new word in my life! It is so much nicer to have a positive take on life instead of, "Oh, no"!

Norm Sharkey

**Daily Reminder
September 30**

Think about it!

I'm lucky if I slept an hour last night! I'm pacing the floor like a caged animal. I'm so paranoid and confused! I know I should stay here but I'm dying for a hit—just enough to help me relax. Who am I kidding? I wouldn't stop at that. As soon as the heat was off, I'd be gone! These people seem to know what they're talking about. They're not just healthcare workers. They have been there! Every minute seems like hours, but I have to hang in there!

FEAR

Trying is good! Doing is better!

Second day and you haven't run yet! Perhaps everyone here is not serious about staying clean, but some are. I'll stay close to them. I may learn . . .

October

Daily Reminder
October 1

Think about it!

Today, I'll get clean! No, tomorrow, because I still have some dope left! I can't just throw it away or give it to someone else! Yeah, tomorrow for sure! Wait! Tomorrow is my second cousin's birthday! I'm

MAYBE

pretty sure it's tomorrow! It wouldn't be right not to celebrate his birthday! I haven't seen him for over a year! I better call him and find out what time I should meet them at the bar! I'll get clean the day after tomorrow! Yeah, that's it!

Trying is good! Doing is better!

That was me for many years! Good intentions? No, just the normal BS I laid on myself for longer than I care to remember! Where are you going?

Norm Sharkey

Daily Reminder
October 2

Think about it!

Many addicts die before the tomorrow when they are going to stop using arrives! Our bodies and minds can only take so much punishment! We always seem to think that when we decide to stop, we can! The cemetery is full of people who thought the same way! I know many people much younger and healthier than I was who didn't make it! When will we tell the dealer not to hit us on seventeen? The odds are not good, folks, and the cards are stacked!

TOO LATE!

Trying is good! Doing is better!

I lost another friend today! He died on his way to the detox center from an overdose! Good intentions, bad timing! In a couple of tomorrows, I'll be at his funeral!

Sanity 365

Daily Reminder
October 3

Think about it!

Sleep! I had four hours sleep last night! I feel a lot better than I did yesterday. I even ate a little last night. I'm still paranoid, but just talking and listening to these people makes me feel less suicidal. They keep telling me I can make it. How I want to believe them. Don't think so much! Leave the street to the street. You're safe here. Leave tomorrow to tomorrow! Another day is almost done!

HANG IN!

Trying is good! Doing is better!

I haven't been drug-free for three straight days for years! Strange! I wonder how much better I will feel tomorrow. I will try to talk more!

Daily Reminder
October 4

Think about it!

I've got a pretty good job, a place to live, and a car! Why do I feel like I'm spinning my wheels? Most people would be happy as hell if they were in my situation! How come I'm not? Sometimes I get all sorts of great ideas and then all of a sudden my head says, "Who are you kidding?" What holds me back from taking a chance? When I'm stoned, I have lots of confidence! When I'm not, I don't! Could drugs be the cause of my euphoria and then my depression?

DECISION

Trying is good! Doing is better!

Is it worth my while to try leaving drugs alone for thirty days, just to see if I would feel any different?

Daily Reminder
October 5

Think about it!

How often have we read in the paper or seen on TV the discovery of the body of a woman or man in an alley? Besides, on the body was a syringe! There has to be a better way to go than that! But for God's grace, it could be you or me! Since it's not, I have to assume there is some unfinished business for us to take care of! The needle does the damage! Can't we deal with our pain in a better way?

PAIN

Trying is good! Doing is better!

Ever hear of quiet desperation? That is how a large number of people live their lives! They are afraid to talk about their pain! Prisoners! Don't be one!

Daily Reminder
October 6

Think about it!

I am amazed! I slept almost the whole night. Already I feel accepted here. I haven't contributed much in group, but the few things I have said have been met with approval. I am starting to feel hungry by mealtime. People talk about their past. I can identify with them. Some have been in and out of recovery several times. Why? Seems like a waste of time if you're not serious. Am I serious? Don't think; you're not equipped!

SERIOUS

Trying is good! Doing is better!

*I have experimented with drugs long enough.
Now I am going to try experimenting with the clean life
by staying clean today!*

Sanity 365

Daily Reminder
October 7

Think about it!

So you've been clean for a while, but you're not that happy! What seems to be the problem, friend? People don't appreciate you? Is that it? They feel you could be doing more?

WHY? Some people are very ungrateful, aren't they? Why should they expect more? After all, you gave up drugs for them and you pay the rent and buy the groceries, as well as clothes for everyone! Since you don't have time for your family because you are attending recovery meetings every night, you'd think they would appreciate you!

Trying is good! Doing is better!

You didn't get clean for them; you got clean for you. However, they count, and it's time you include them in your recovery! We are family!

Norm Sharkey

Daily Reminder
October 8

Think about it!

Anyone who has had some sort of religious upbringing may or may not enjoy hearing the word God! If the experience was negative, don't blame poor old God! He always gets screamed at instead of the people who introduced you to Him. Or perhaps some of the fault may have been yours and mine! We weren't exactly super students of His either, so let's give God a little bit of credit, shall we? He did, after all, keep you alive so you could get clean! Or are you alive? Just kidding!

SMILE!

Trying is good! Doing is better!
---

*Let's face it; God must have a sense of humor if
He put up with us guys all these years!
How about us getting one?*

Sanity 365

**Daily Reminder
October 9**

Think about it!

I woke up this morning feeling much better physically and mentally. I think the atmosphere around here is starting to rub off on me. More and more, I can see the people who are serious and the people who are not. I want to be included with the serious ones. I have heard the expression, "Losers are just winners who aren't ready yet." I really think I am ready—in fact, I know I am. Let's get on with the day!

REAL!

Trying is good! Doing is better!

I talked about some things today I have kept hidden all my life. I feel a lot better as a result. I'm going to continue talking about . . .

Norm Sharkey

Daily Reminder
October 10

Think about it!

On one episode of the TV program Cheers, Norm came in on a cold day, and Woody said, "Hi Mr. Peterson, Jack Frost nipping at your nose?" Norm said, "Yeah, now let's get Joe Beer nipping at my liver!" That was a great line, but the reality is many alcohol drinkers die from liver problems! Many pot smokers die from the unfiltered smoke damage to their lungs! We have notices on cigarette packs about the danger to our health from smoking filtered cigarettes and we have people campaigning to legalize unfiltered pot. What's wrong with this picture?

NO PROBLEM

Trying is good! Doing is better!

Pot's harmless; you don't get addicted! I know—the same way I can't get addicted to sugar, ice cream, sex . . .

Daily Reminder
October 11

Think about it!

COMING DOWN!

Well, I woke up this morning in a terrible mood; you talk about a person with the "coming down" blues! This is when everyone in my little circle walks very, very quietly! The so-called head of the house is not well! When he arrived through the door at 3:00 a.m., he was not too concerned about anyone else's well-being! Everything was fun and games at that hour because he was happy! Happy! He couldn't understand where everyone's sense of humor was. A tip to the wise: don't remind him of that this morning!

Trying is good! Doing is better!

To the families of addicts—for your own health, if there is anything to eat for breakfast, eat it quickly and get the hell out of the house, now! Get out before the addict gets up and starts demanding your blood!

Norm Sharkey

**Daily Reminder
October 12**

Think about it!

In the first few days of a person's recovery they often say, "I very seldom drank alcohol. Drugs were my problem. If I stop using drugs, does that mean I can drink alcohol?" Our answer: the Canadian and American Medical Associations say alcohol is a drug. Our first value says that we are powerless over any kind of drug. We have seen people who drank alcohol after being clean for a while and either became alcoholics or returned to drugs. Russian roulette, anyone?

ADDICTIVES

Trying is good! Doing is better!

Value three says that if I change me, I will not need drugs. Today, I will work on changing my impatience!

Sanity 365

Daily Reminder
October 13

Think about it!

People keep telling me that if I just ask God to come into my life, He will! But why would He after the crap I threw His way most of my life? They tell me that is the difference between God and people! People

PEOPLE! GOD!

get even; God just keeps on loving us! When we get clean, it is awful hard to look back over our lives and still be able to love ourselves! Chances are good that not too many people love us either! We have to trust what others are saying and give God a shot! We need love!

Trying is good! Doing is better!

To find God, the Bible says we have to be like little children! If that's the case, most of us should have no trouble connecting, right?

293

Daily Reminder
October 14

Think about it!

So I'm clean! I've finally made an effort to communicate with God, as I don't understand Him! Just suppose He is listening to me when I ask for help this morning! What exactly should I expect? You say you asked for help! Then He will give you the strength to cope with anything that comes up today! That doesn't mean He'll do your day's work for you; He will give you the strength to do your own work and stay clean! If that's what you honestly ask for, then that's what you'll get!

BE REAL!

Trying is good! Doing is better!

Don't play games with God by asking for one thing when you want something else! Place your order with Him and watch Him deliver!

Sanity 365

**Daily Reminder
October 15**

Think about it!

We also have people who had alcohol as their problem who thought they could pop a few pills or smoke a few joints. They ended up on the bottle again. We believe

ESCAPE

if you need any artificial substance to give you confidence and love yourself, then you have an addiction problem. If you are a different person when you are using than you are when you're not, you answer your own question. In the end, you have to convince you, not us.

Trying is good! Doing is better!

We always look for an escape hatch, but there is none! Instead of trying to escape, I will look at what I'm trying to escape from!

Daily Reminder
October 16

Think about it!

These little reminders are useless unless you are in the mood to be reminded! If everything you read each day doesn't hit a nerve of some sort, then perhaps this is the wrong book for you! We are talking here to people who have tried drugs as a way of life and found they don't live up to the hype! These reminders are not meant to be our horoscope, just a daily gut check to hopefully start your day on a positive note!

LOOK

Trying is good! Doing is better!

If fear has you ready to throw up, ask God, as you may or may not understand Him, to give you the strength to cope. Keep on asking, not just once!

Daily Reminder
October 17

Think about it!

Man it's good to be clean! There was a time in my life when I couldn't have said that! Clean! Who wants to be clean? I thought that would be the most boring, dead way of living there was! I almost discovered the dead part but not because I was clean! I understand now what being born again means—a chance to really live the way I was meant to! I hope if you are reading this today, you are shouting, "Right on!"

ALIVE

Trying is good! Doing is better!
---

*If you are still using and enjoying drugs,
I doubt if you got much out of what you just finished
reading! Sorry about that!*

Norm Sharkey

***Daily Reminder
October 18***

Think about it!

Years ago, addicts were just thrown into jail. There were no detox or rehab programs. They would be brought in front of a judge, given a fine or jail time, and told not to do it again. Society thought these people had the power to change! We know differently! When we start, we can't stop until someone or something stops us. On our own, the fight is hopeless. We need help!

NO POWER

Trying is good! Doing is better!

We would like to feel that we don't have to depend on other people for help. Many have tried but failed! Today I will remove my ego and ask for help by letting people know who I am!

Daily Reminder
October 19

Think about it!

I have a big problem today! What big problem did I have on this day five years ago? I have no idea, but I'm sure there was something at that time I was positive I could never find an answer for! Whatever it was, I survived it, and I can survive today's problem too! So can you, folks!

ANSWERS

Unless you're about to be executed, there are always answers! Perhaps we don't like the answer, but there are answers!

Trying is good! Doing is better!

All my life, I looked for the easy way out! I found that the easy way out was to face the problem and accept the solution! Are you nuts?

Norm Sharkey

Daily Reminder
October 20

Think about it!

LIVING

What about yesterday's problem or problems? What did I do about them? Sit, think, and worry or get some advice, pray about it, and tackle it? If I make an effort to do something, even if the results were not what I wanted, at least I did something! If I just sit and think and hope that the problem will disappear, I will soon disappear back into the drug world! I have to understand that when I am clean, I am responsible for my own life! When I am stoned, drugs are responsible, but I pay the price!

Trying is good! Doing is better!

I have grown up in many ways since I got clean, but I still see life with the amazement of a little child! There is so much to discover, folks!

Daily Reminder
October 21

Think about it!

If you are serious about staying clean, you will need help from more than just people. God as you come to know God will also need to be part of it. Our second value says, "Through being open and honest with each other, we came to know God!" You may have had some bad experiences with God, people, but we are not here to shove God down your throat. Your relationship with God will come as you get more open and honest with people!

GET REAL

Trying is good! Doing is better!

I do have a problem with God, but I also know that I want to stay clean. I will take your advice, and today, I will be open and honest with everyone I meet!

Norm Sharkey

Daily Reminder
October 22

Think about it!

Patience and faith! In my case, these are two of the most valuable assets I have been given by the God of my understanding! I am fortunate enough to have lived clean a good number of years, one day at a time, and over time, I improved my ability to apply, with God's help, both patience and faith on a daily basis. If I believe that there are answers, and with work on my part, if I allow God the time necessary to produce those answers, life will unfold as it should for me!

TRUST

Trying is good! Doing is better!

I am no more special than you are—in fact, I may be less special than you! Patience and faith will work for anyone, even you!

Daily Reminder
October 23

Think about it!

When we decide to get clean—I mean seriously decide to get clean—drugs are no longer our problem! Living without drugs and finding our way in society now becomes our goal! How do we fit in with the people **YOU AND ME** who cope each day with life with no need to get stoned over it? My only problem is me! Your only problem is you! I have no control over what other people do, and neither do you! I need to change my attitude, and you need to change yours!

Trying is good! Doing is better!

I must stop blaming everyone around me! Stop it! Stop it! Stop it! Stop it! Stop it! Get it?

Norm Sharkey

**Daily Reminder
October 24**

Think about it!

Many people, when it comes to drugs, take the attitude, "I could die tomorrow, so I may as well enjoy life while I can!" No one knows how long they will live, but how much do we really enjoy life when we aren't aware of what's really happening most of the time? That's not enjoying life; that's just avoiding reality! Learning how to deal with reality is a life skill we can't acquire while we are stoned! Drugs make all our decisions! Ever wonder why some of your decisions have been so poor?

REALITY

Trying is good! Doing is better!

The longer we avoid reality, the more paranoid we become just thinking about it! Just because you're not paranoid doesn't mean they're not after you!

Sanity 365

**Daily Reminder
October 25**

Think about it!

GUILT

None of us are or will become perfect! We can, however, live quite happily without drugs and make contributions toward making this world a better place to live! I have a hard time contributing anything positive if I am not happy myself! One thing that will rob me of happiness is guilt! Whatever causes the guilt has to go if I am to be happy and productive in this life! If I am not happy and productive while I am filled with guilt, it won't be long before I am filled with drugs!

Trying is good! Doing is better!

Perhaps unknowingly we used drugs to kill guilt and as a result of our drug use, created more guilt! That's why we stayed stoned! What must I do to get rid of guilt and stay happy clean?

Daily Reminder
October 26

Think about it!

If I am clean today but not very happy, whose fault is it? All my life, I was an expert at putting the blame on something or someone else, so where do I place the blame now? This is my life, so if I am not happy, then it's my fault! Oh God no! It can't be my fault! I like to take the credit when things are good, so why not take the blame when things are bad? Am I living for today? Am I working at my recovery today?

BLAME

Trying is good! Doing is better!

Life is very short, and if I waste today being bummed out, I'm a fool! Didn't I waste enough days when I was using? I can feel better today if I help someone else feel better today! Today! Today! Today!

Sanity 365

Daily Reminder
October 27

Think about it!

None of us has arrived at perfection's destination! I sure haven't, anyhow, but life is good! You may be saying, "Don't make me puke!" I, too, said that at one point, so you're not alone! You are, however, listening to the wrong people if that's how you feel! You may not win the lottery jackpot tonight, but if you stay clean and get a little honest, you'll avoid all the jackpots you have been in up to now!

POOR ME

Trying is good! Doing is better!

Ever hear of the power of negative thinking? It was written by all the drug addicts who died stoned!

Norm Sharkey

**Daily Reminder
October 28**

Think about it!

Thinking positively does not mean we live in a shell, pretending all is well with the world! There are many problems about which you and I can do nothing! Reality check! However, I can do something about my own little world and my stinking attitude toward life! Sitting on my balcony and looking down on everyone and everything does not make me or the world any better! Perhaps if I cut you some slack, the world will cut me some slack! I believe it's time!

FORGIVE

Trying is good! Doing is better!

Why am I waiting for the world to stop fighting when I'm sitting here with a loaded gun? I dunno!

Daily Reminder
October 29

Think about it!

I got clean because I didn't want to die stoned! Selfish reason, eh? Now I don't want to die because I would like to help as many people as I can to get out of the hamster's wheel! This clean life just keeps getting better and better! The amazing thing, as long as I stay clean, is I can't seem to screw it up! I've tried, but I can't! It looks like God has decided that I have work to do, so He won't let me screw it up!

GO ON!

Trying is good! Doing is better!

One person helping one other person and so on and so on is how we can clean up our cities, folks! Let it begin with you!

Daily Reminder
October 30

Think about it!

We always think we are the only ones with problems and that our problems are worse than anyone could imagine! Poor us! I've seen people with terminal illnesses and you would think they don't know what a problem is! What is the difference between us and them? We seem to be chronic whiners! We are little kids with our diapers full and just sitting in them! We can't stand the smell, but we won't do anything about it either! It is time to grow up and take off those stinky diapers!

CHANGE

Trying is good! Doing is better!

Flush the drugs, and flush the diapers that go with drugs! It's time to stand up and start living!

Daily Reminder
October 31

Think about it!

I used to ask my mother, "What do you want for Christmas, Mom?" She would say, "Good kids!" I'm sure that's what most moms would like! Just like my mom, not too many got what they wanted, did

SELFISH

they? I gave my mom four boxes of Cracker Jacks for her birthday when I was a kid. I knew she didn't like them and would give them back to me! She did! Can you see how these life skills allowed me to become a first-class drug addict? Don't give anybody anything unless you get something back, right?

Trying is good! Doing is better!

Before the sun goes down tonight, try to make someone's life a little bit easier! C'mon, you can think of something!

November

**Daily Reminder
November 1**

Think about it!

Some addicts have had periods of time where they were clean, but something always seemed to be missing in their lives! They thought, Life is good. I have a decent job, a good partner, a car, and a home, but still something is missing! Life without drugs seemed to leave a hole! As long as people think drugs will fill the hole, they will eventually go back to using! As long as the good times linger in our minds, we will return to drugs, looking for them!

DAYDREAM!

Trying is good! Doing is better!

There is no denying that drugs can give you a high that happy clean has a difficult time competing with! The difference is that happy clean is free and real but requires work on yourself!

Daily Reminder
November 2

Think about it!

DECISIONS

Chasing the high in drugs leads to an early grave or a lockup! Chasing the high in happy clean leads to an adventure that drugs can only promise! The drug high is the result of amusing yourself while abusing yourself and many other people! The happy clean high is the result of changing from selfish to selfless, dishonest to honest, hateful to loving! The drug high requires using drugs and people; the happy clean high requires self-examination and helping people! It's your move!

Trying is good! Doing is better!

If the only times life feels good are stoned times, then you have a problem! Why do you feel you don't have what it takes to enjoy life without drugs? Ever get serious about these questions?

Daily Reminder
November 3

Think about it!

There are many positives that lead to happy clean and many negatives that lead to happy stoned! If you have used drugs for a while, you know the happy stoned negatives! For me, the happy clean positives

HAPPY WHAT? include feeling useful, not useless! Helping others gives me that useful feeling even if I don't see the results I'm hoping for! The important thing is that I give it my best and my motives are pure! I could not say that when I was using! How about you, pilgrim?

Trying is good! Doing is better!

You can find the contentment you are searching for if you only put the Great Spirit first, your neighbor second, and great, grand, and wonderful you next!

Norm Sharkey

Daily Reminder
November 4

Think about it!

Feeling useful through helping others will only carry us so far! Unless we are examining and changing our own selves, we will eventually run out of the help we are trying to pass on to others! There will come a time when the help we are giving doesn't have the same spark it had when we first started! This is where the unseen divine help refuels us and allows us to see that we can only do so much on our own strength!

ALONE?

Trying is good! Doing is better!

Each of us has to walk our own spiritual walk!
Many people can help us on our journey,
but each of us has to do our own walking!
Have you started yet? Happy hiking!

Sanity 365

**Daily Reminder
November 5**

Think about it!

Most of us, when we do connect with this mysterious power, tend to get a little preachy or pushy! We can see that others aren't as turned on with life as we feel we are, and we are determined to save them! I am sorry to say that over the years, I got these two things mixed up! For any people I tried to save instead of love, I hope you can forgive me and allow me the opportunity to love you! My only job is to love and let God do the "save" part!

LOVE

Trying is good! Doing is better!

*God says, "Love your neighbor,"
not save your neighbor!*

317

Norm Sharkey

**Daily Reminder
November 6**

Think about it!

Man, every day I hear of good friends I had who have gone back to search for happy stoned! Many are dead or locked up, and many are on the verge of the same! As I said, I can't save anyone, but I sure would like **AGAIN!** the chance to love these friends one more time! If you know any or you are one, please visit our website, Sanity365.com! Give us and you a chance to do it right this time! We all are guilty of mistakes, folks. No one—least of all me—has done everything perfectly since getting clean!

Trying is good! Doing is better!

How comfortable do we feel when we ignore someone else's pain? Makes for an unfulfilled day, doesn't it?

Sanity 365

Daily Reminder
November 7

Think about it!

Many, many people have contributed to me being able to live happy clean! They all know who they are, God knows who they are, and most importantly, I know who they are! If you are happy clean, I'm sure you can say

SHARING!

the same thing! I believe that when I share with someone, I receive much more than I share! If you're as selfish as I am, how can you beat that deal? You can't! However, start sharing and stop receiving!

Trying is good! Doing is better!

Sanity 365 is important to me for the simple reason that it gives me a chance to share! I stop growing or certainly slow down my growth when I stop sharing! How about you?

Norm Sharkey

**Daily Reminder
November 8**

Think about it!

I believe that when my gearshift is in drive and I'm at the speed limit, then I am fully alive! Moving forward looking for hitchhikers who want to find their way home is the secret to a good trip! How many people have I driven past lately? Many I may pick up won't have the same destination as mine or yours, but they deserve to hear where we are going! We can tell them and let them make up their own minds if it is for them!

JUMP IN!

Trying is good! Doing is better!

On the road of life, there are drivers and there are passengers. Which are you?

Daily Reminder
November 9

Think about it!

At the beginning of our drug-using career, we looked for excuses to get stoned! "All my friends are users! Who wants to be like all the boring people I see? I want to enjoy life! No one cares about me anyway! Life is full of crap anyway!" There is no end to the excuses! As our careers continued, we just got stoned—no need for excuses! This was going to be our life from now on! We found it easier to lose than to win! Or did we?

REAL?

Trying is good! Doing is better!

As long as we think losing is easier than winning, we will continue to lose! We have to stop lying to ourselves! In our guts, we know we would rather win! It takes work! Work! Honesty! Work!

Daily Reminder
November 10

Think about it!

In this country, governments at all levels make things easy for us to stay sick! Money for drugs (called Social Assistance), food banks, free clothes, free needles, and even free drugs are available in some communities. I didn't say everyone on Social Assistance is an addict, but there are many addicts collecting! There is no argument that addiction is a disease! Why are governments mostly concerned with the physical aspect of the disease? Without help for the mental and spiritual aspects, we will just be physically healthy users!

ENABLERS

Trying is good! Doing is better!

There are many of us wandering the streets in this country and countries around the world in great shape physically but with nothing left mentally or spiritually! We have helped to create that!

Sanity 365

**Daily Reminder
November 11**

Think about it!

On this day around the world, many people gather to remember the people who gave up their lives so you and I could live in a free society! That doesn't mean there is freedom everywhere, but the people who died did their best to make it free! There are people in free societies who are not free! They are imprisoned by drugs! People have offered to get them out of their prison, but they insist they enjoy being locked up! How about you, inmate? Are you enjoying your segregation from the real world?

FREE!

Trying is good! Doing is better!

Even when we are offered a chance to escape the burning barn, we react just like horses and run back in! Are we more comfortable there?

323

Norm Sharkey

**Daily Reminder
November 12**

Think about it!

Experts can show us physically and mentally what drugs are and will do to us, and we still say, "Who cares?" There are many people who really are concerned about what happens to us, and we know it and we still say, "Who cares?" For close friends and family, our attitudes and actions cause pain, fear, and anguish every day! We continue to say, "Who cares?" We certainly won't admit it, but we enjoy having the power to control other people's lives like we do! Every day they say, "What can we do to help?" but we say, "Who cares?"

I CARE!

Trying is good! Doing is better!

Watch out that you don't yell, "Fire!" one time too many! Perhaps your next ambulance ride will be your last!

Sanity 365

Daily Reminder
November 13

Think about it!

At the beginning of our drug use, we were looking, and we found a solution for the emotional pain in our lives! Whether the pain was real or imagined doesn't matter!

FRIENDS!

We just wanted relief! We found it to a degree, and someone turned us on to something even better! We felt that this friend was the most caring, understanding person we had ever met! Then we met someone who turned us on to something even better! So now, the message in our minds was clear! Friends are people who make you feel good! Enemies are people who try to take away your friends! Enemies are family, social workers, police etc.!

Trying is good! Doing is better!

As you continue into hell, do you ever wonder if you may have come to understand things a little backward? Are your friends still your friends and your enemies still your enemies?

Norm Sharkey

**Daily Reminder
November 14**

Think about it!

There is no argument that many of us come from messed-up families! This can certainly make us targets for dope! I have, however, met people from more messed-up families than I came from, and they did not turn to dope! People with guts make up their minds early in their lives that they will escape the insanity—and they do! Even though we say, "I will never be like my father!" that is exactly what we become! Then, when we realize we are carbon copies, we say, "What do you expect? I'm just doing what I was shown!" That was my favorite excuse!

EXCUSES

Trying is good! Doing is better!

The day that I couldn't believe my own excuses was the day I seriously asked for help! I haven't used since then! Try it!

Sanity 365

Daily Reminder
November 15

Think about it!

Believe me, when the excuses go, the help just keeps coming and coming and coming! The old enemies become the new friends! Isn't it amazing how people change? What took those people so long to understand and love you? It seems we are suddenly rescued from the lost and found department! We stop fighting with everyone and everything! What the hell is going on? Is it possible I was wrong? Why is everyone being so nice to me? What trick are they about to pull on me?

AMAZED!

Trying is good! Doing is better!

There's no trick, friend! What you see and feel is what you'll get as long as you avoid the old excuses! Remember that word you discarded years ago, honesty?

Norm Sharkey

Daily Reminder
November 16

Think about it!

Did you ever think you would say and believe, "It's good to be clean?" Regardless of material things, can you say, "Man do I feel good! Am I dreaming?" No, no, no, no, no! Pinch yourself—it's real!

GRATEFUL

Gratitude for a good sleep! Gratitude for the food I just ate! Gratitude for real people who I never thought I could stomach! Gratitude for being alive! Gratitude for gratitude! I am so fortunate; luck had nothing to do with it! The people and the Great Spirit are responsible for today's opportunities! Thank you both!

Trying is good! Doing is better!

*The more gratitude I have and give to others,
the more it multiplies in me and them!
Let my attitude be one of gratitude!*

Sanity 365

Daily Reminder
November 17

Think about it!

Why is society so eager to keep us sick? As I have mentioned several times already, we are given free food, free healthcare (which we abuse), free needles, free methadone, and now even free heroin in some communities! If I am a using addict and I am receiving all these benefits, how motivated will I be to get clean? I may have to go to work! I may have to be responsible for my own life for a change! What a shocker!

GIVE ME!

Trying is good! Doing is better!

Do I want to be treated like a little child all my life? In the above situation, isn't that the role the government is playing in my life by enabling my dependence on it?

Norm Sharkey

Daily Reminder
November 18

Think about it!

AM I?

I'm sick, I'm sick, I'm very, very, sick! I'm sick, I'm sick I'm very, very, sick! Until I really believed that, I had no hope of any lasting abstinence! As long as I thought I wasn't as bad as some others, I stayed sick! I told people I wanted help, but the only help I wanted was all the free stuff! I knew my life didn't have to be the way it was, but I had lost confidence in my ability to be responsible for me!

Trying is good! Doing is better!

I believe, and this is just my own opinion, the Great Spirit of the universe knows when we are completely ready to change and reaches down and gives us the strength to do it!

Sanity 365

Daily Reminder
November 19

Think about it!

Love is patient! The people in our lives who stand by helplessly waiting for us to receive the love they are offering are the real heroes in this world! The pain they endure while they watch us slowly killing ourselves is the pain that only heroes can handle! Patience and faith, both delivered by the Great Spirit, make up their survival kits! How many nights have they spent on their knees waiting for us to fall through the door, hoping the phone will ring and also hoping it won't? Fear!

HELPLESS

Trying is good! Doing is better!

What sort of masochistic animals are we that we put these people through this torture? How will you react if you have to go through the same someday?

Norm Sharkey

Daily Reminder
November 20

Think about it!

Is there a human being in this world who could convince us to humiliate ourselves for all those years? I don't think anyone alive could control us like drugs did! The insane thing was that we realized this and went **BEAT ME!** on anyway! Beat me! Beat me! I'm no good! Isn't that what I was saying to drugs? Drugs were only too willing to deliver the beating! How lost could I have been to actually think I was having fun?

Trying is good! Doing is better!

Out of all the addicts in this world, and there are many, only a small percentage will live long enough to get happy clean! Many will go back to using rather than do the necessary work to reach the goal!

Daily Reminder
November 21

Think about it!

Love is kind! Do people love us when they knowingly accept our lies and behavior? I'm sure they think they do, but they would be saving us a lot of wasted time if they had just told us we were full of it! They had to eventually tell us in order to get our attention, but it's a shame they waited so long! I'm not blaming them; I'm sure they thought they were helping! When my ass hits the cement instead of a cushion, I may think about doing something for me!

BOTTOM!

Trying is good! Doing is better!

I am one who was fortunate enough to hit the cement and was able to get up and walk to freedom! Many won't! Will you?

Norm Sharkey

Daily Reminder
November 22

Think about it!

Love is not envious! I used to say, "I envy him or her!" I don't say that anymore! Mostly I envied the material things they had! I now understand that material things are the easiest of all things in life to acquire! Determination and hard work will deliver them! What I should have been envious of is a person's positive character and morals! I can always acquire these attributes, but they involve a closer relationship with the Great Spirit who delivers them upon request!

WORK!

Trying is good! Doing is better!

I learned that instead of being envious of anyone, I only had to get rid of the negatives in my character and ask God to help me replace them with positives!

Daily Reminder
November 23

Think about it!

Love is not boastful! I cannot boast or brag about my success in staying clean! Happy clean is simply the end result of being grateful for the gifts the Great Spirit has freely given me! As long as I give Him the glory and let Him do any boasting in my regard, I will remain humble and able to love people! After all, what have I got to boast or brag about? I didn't want to die; I asked for His help, and He delivered! End of story!

PRAISE!

Trying is good! Doing is better!

The old me would gladly brag about the new me, but the new me knows where the credit belongs!

Daily Reminder
November 24

Think about it!

Love is not arrogant or rude! When I was using, I was both arrogant and rude, along with a number of other negative defects. Being arrogant and rude are two absolute necessities if you want to be a successful drug addict! Until you developed these skills, you were not fully accepted into the drug culture! By the time we reached full-blown addiction, these two skills were complete aspects of our own makeup! These were the skills we used to keep people who wanted to help us at arm's length!

LIFE SKILLS!

Trying is good! Doing is better!

Addicts hate the word goof, but that is just another word for arrogant and rude! Addicts think they are the most intelligent people on earth, so goof is a very insulting word to them!

Daily Reminder
November 25

Think about it!

Love is not irritable! Irritated—that was me most of the time when I wasn't totally stoned! Everyone and everything in this world bothered me! I, of course,

CONFUSED?

didn't see that mostly I was irritated with myself! We are great at finding other things and people we can blame for our situations! That is how we managed to stay sick! Why do addicts feel they are right and the whole world is wrong? I guess it is because we have had so much success in life, eh?

Trying is good! Doing is better!

If only the world could understand me! What about if I only could understand myself? Forget it; pass the joint!

Norm Sharkey

**Daily Reminder
November 26**

Think about it!

Love is not resentful. There's no better example of resentment than a drug addict, either stoned or at various stages of recovery! We have made a fine art out of resentment! No human being does it better! We have more resentment in our memory banks than most up-to-date computers!

GOSSIP?

Resentment seems to give us our reason for living! Resentment gives us the excuse we need to avoid looking at ourselves! Gossip is the fuel that keeps resentment burning. If you want to measure how well someone's recovery is going, just listen to how much they chop someone up behind their back! Check the mirror!

Trying is good! Doing is better!

When I fall into gossip, I go backward in my growth. I become the immature little person I was most of my life! I want to move into post-secondary and onward!

Sanity 365

**Daily Reminder
November 27**

Think about it!

Love rejoices in the truth! Could that be why I had so much trouble loving myself and others? Honesty is involved! This was an ingredient in my makeup that practically disappeared! The truth will set you free! The truth will allow me to discover love! All those years, I buried my conscience in lies and worked hard at keeping God as far away as I could! I guess as long as I wasn't entirely insensitive, God was able to reach me through what little conscience I had left and allowed me to understand that there was hope!

TRUTH?

Trying is good! Doing is better!

Today, I will love people and myself by being completely honest with them and me! This is the answer to contentment and love!

Norm Sharkey

Daily Reminder
November 28

Think about it!

Love hopes all things! Simply, love gives us hope! That does not mean I hope this or I hope that; it means love gives us a purpose, a reason for living! Hate gives us a purpose or reason for killing and hurting! I **HOPE** don't know which requires the most energy, but I do know that I feel a lot better when I love! I was thirty-four years old when I got clean. I'm seventy-four years old at this moment, so roughly half of my life was spent in hating! For the last forty years, I've been doing my best to love! It's getting easier, folks!

Trying is good! Doing is better!

When I do not love people, I'm wasting valuable time that the Great Spirit is freely giving me! If I want to really live, I have to really love!

Daily Reminder
November 29

Think about it!

Love endures all things! In my opinion, the perfect example of that is Jesus on the cross saying, "Father forgive them, they don't know what they're doing!" We still don't! Even when we're happy clean, we don't spend any of our time in gossip or resentment! The people in our lives who put up with our crap for so long are another example of love's endurance! Any time you think you'll stop loving someone, just look at the people who refused to give up on you!

HANG IN

Happy birthday, Anna!
Trying is good! Doing is better!

Jesus and the people in our lives are the examples of guts that we must develop if we want to live well in this life!

Norm Sharkey

Daily Reminder
November 30

Think about it!

Love never ends! The world has tried throughout history to kill love, and some days it almost appears to be succeeding! Then along come a few little innocent kids with joy and happiness on their faces and love comes alive again. We all have to return to the day when we felt like that and start building our lives the loving way! Even if you are positive you had no happy days as a child, start building your life the way you would have wanted it to be! There are so many people in this world who would want to have that opportunity. We have it, so get moving! Pass the results on to others, and really begin to live!

FOREVER

Trying is good! Doing is better!

If God sees the little sparrow fall, don't you think He's aware of us stumbling around? He loves hearing from strangers, so give Him a call!

December

Daily Reminder
December 1

Think about it!

Some people may try pot on the insistence of their friends and discover they don't like the feeling they got! Chances are good that these people also don't like the high that comes from a few drinks of alcohol!

NO WAY!

They will quite likely not develop an addiction to any drug! Then there are people like me and you! That high was the beginning of life for us! Pot and alcohol were just the start of our "incredible journey" to insanity or death!

Trying is good! Doing is better!

I guess that until the medical profession can develop tests to determine who may or may not become addicted, prisons, mental institutions, and graveyards are where a lot of us will arrive!

Norm Sharkey

Daily Reminder
December 2

Think about it!

With all the insanity, killing, and hatred in today's society, why is there no curriculum in our education system to show people how to live happily without being introduced to drugs? You may say, "That should be done at home!" But let's face it, it's not or we wouldn't have so many kids turning to dope! We have breakfast programs for kids who aren't getting fed at home, and no one seems to think that's an invasion of the family unit. So what about happiness lessons?

ALONE

Trying is good! Doing is better!

The kids in the breakfast programs, I think you would agree, are not getting a lot of other things at home if they can't even get breakfast! You tell us the answer!

Daily Reminder
December 3

Think about it!

SOCIAL USER

Even if a successful prevention program started today, fifty years would probably pass before addiction could be stamped out! We are looking for cures for heart disease, cancer, and AIDS when addiction is related to all of these! Why doesn't anyone ever talk about finding a cure for addiction? Would that put too many people out of work? Just consider how many bars or liquor outlets you would need if the only customers were true social drinkers. One or two drinks every few weeks is the consumption of the true social drinker! Surprised?

Trying is good! Doing is better!

There are greater minds than mine out there; maybe a discussion among you could produce some answers! Our solutions so far don't seem to be giving results!

Daily Reminder
December 4

Think about it!

I guess until we find a foolproof recovery program, finding a prevention program is a long way off! It looks like society is content with having the car hit the tree before any work can be done! The world asks, "What can be done?" I don't know, but I think it's time to start looking! Don't you? We read every day about car theft. How come no one seems to talk about the reason for the car theft? Certainly organized crime is making money, but the people stealing the cars are usually addicts. Why do they not mention this in the news?

THEFT

Trying is good! Doing is better!

The authorities tell us that the car thieves are the same ones doing it over and over! When they are sentenced to time, why are there no assessments of their drug use?

Daily Reminder
December 5

Think about it!

PREVENTION

We who are addicted, what can we do to make sure we don't use again? At this point, even though we may want to, we can't save the world! What about making sure we save ourselves? We are now aware that we can one day at a time! So, what can I do today to stay happy clean? The first thing for me is to be grateful I am alive! Many of my family members and friends are not alive because of drugs! I start today by thanking God! How about you?

Trying is good! Doing is better!

Perhaps you don't want to thank God! If you are alive and clean, it seems to me someone deserves some thanks!

Daily Reminder
December 6

Think about it!

If I wake up in a lousy mood, it's obvious that my gratitude has gone south! Why? Family, work, finances, what? Perhaps all three are involved, but does that mean I shouldn't be grateful I'm not stoned? Am I the reason these three areas of my life are not functioning properly? I'm sure I have a lot to do with it! I can't use any of these as an excuse to avoid my responsibilities. Today I can stay clean, happy, and grateful as long as I face the problems honestly and unafraid. Will I?

DECISIONS

Trying is good! Doing is better!

With God and my friends I have the power to make a lousy day into a very rewarding day! It's my choice! And the winner is?

Daily Reminder
December 7

Think about it!

When anything bothered me, I talked about it! As time has passed, my ability to do this has improved! I still waste too much time going over and over things in my own mind looking for answers when all need to do is talk to someone! I get so caught up in my own ego that I don't even ask God because I think I can figure it out! Then I call on the old bush league pinch hitter as a last resort! He usually says, "Call someone who has experience with this problem." Simple, eh?

TALK

Trying is good! Doing is better!

How much time have you wasted today? Perhaps, like me, you know the answer to your problem. You just don't want to accept the answer, huh?

Norm Sharkey

Daily Reminder
December 8

Think about it!

I create most of my problems! Also, most of my problems are not problems! Sometimes I think if I have problems, this will make me look important, because only important people have problems! Do you follow? When I was stoned, I was a walking problem! When I am clean, I get a chance to sit down and look for solutions! If every day I have a problem, especially the same one, I had better get some help! Where's the elevator? I'm tired of climbing the stairs!

ANSWERS!

Trying is good! Doing is better!

God and my friends act as the elevator for me! What does it for you?

Sanity 365

Daily Reminder
December 9

Think about it!

How much time would I save when I have a crisis if I went to God immediately instead of the never-ending roller coaster of thinking? This is the same person who, when he was stoned, who could not think of anything but staying stoned! Why do I suddenly think I'm a genius with all the answers for myself? Beats me! Without even realizing it, I set off to solve my problem with no tools, not even a screwdriver! I'm going to solve them though!

TOOLS?

Trying is good! Doing is better!

Friend! What's in your toolkit today? Don't head out with an empty box! It could be a long, hard day if you do! This is the voice of experience talking!

Daily Reminder
December 10

Think about it!

It seems like all the wasted days and wasted nights were necessary for me to arrive at my destination! Drugs gave me an excuse! What about today? What excuse do I have if today is not productive? Who can I blame, or what should I blame? There must be someone or something, right? Wrong! I've run out of excuses? Impossible! It can't be me! It is, friend! It is! If I think like a loser, I will be a loser! I would rather be a winner.

ASK

Trying is good! Doing is better!

Garbage in, garbage out! Who can change that cycle? I can, and you can! Now! Today! Do it!

Sanity 365

***Daily Reminder**
December 11*

Think about it!

THINK!

What excuse could I find to get stoned today? Man I hate that word excuse! It makes me sound like a wimp! Well? There are no reasons! There are lots of excuses though! I could use one of many that are stored in my memory bank! They are all just excuses! Real people don't look for excuses; they look for answers. Real people stand their ground and face the problem! Real people are made out of blood and guts—not dope! Are you real people? Of course you are! You're here!

Trying is good! Doing is better!

Are your friends on a mission or still spinning their wheels? How much time do you have to achieve your goals? What is your goal? Don't know?

Norm Sharkey

**Daily Reminder
December 12**

Think about it!

There are days, many, many days, when I feel so good, I wish I could grab a microphone and yell, "Norm to earth, Norm to earth!" Try this routine, just for today! Love God! Love your neighbor! Love yourself!

ENERGY

Can you hear me now loud and clear? Are we having fun yet? I know I'm whacked, but I'm whacked with love instead of hate! I feel I have enough energy to tear this whole apartment building down and then rebuild it! That's not the coffee either!

Trying is good! Doing is better!

If there's anyone else out there who feels that way, get in touch! It's time to start making some changes before the world blows up!

Daily Reminder
December 13

Think about it!

We keep asking the Great Spirit if He has any new answers for our world! He says, "You have the answers; make them work!" As an addict, I wanted to use drugs and still be successful! While the world, it seems, wants peace, we continue to hate each other! As a recovering addict, I have six simple things to do to stay happy clean! If I don't do them, I may still stay clean, but I won't be happy clean!

LIVING

Trying is good! Doing is better!

Being anything other than happy clean doesn't appeal to me! If just being clean is good enough for you, lots of luck!

Daily Reminder
December 14

Think about it!

HEROES

Can you think of someone you would like to be the same as? Who and why? Don't freak out now, but my hero would be Jesus! All His beliefs and attributes are things that really appeal to me! He said that we can do anything if we ask the Father and persist in doing it! When I think like Him, I feel good! When I act like Him, I feel even better! That's where the similarities end! I do it sporadically; He did it every day of His short life!

Trying is good! Doing is better!

We all need someone to look up to! Who have you seen who looks pretty content? Ask him or her what his or her secret is!

Daily Reminder
December 15

Think about it!

GOOD LIFE!

I don't know about you, but even on my best happy clean days, I don't overextend myself when it comes to changing negative habits and attitudes! I know from experience that the more I change, the better I feel, yet I don't consider myself a slave driver! I often wonder how good I could feel if I was! I will probably never find out, because I'm too lazy! Having said that, life has been more than terrific clean!

Trying is good! Doing is better!

If you have been clean awhile and you're not content 95 percent of the time, what's keeping you clean? Talk to someone quick!

Norm Sharkey

**Daily Reminder
December 16**

Think about it!

Most of the time when I was using, my face looked like nine days of rain! If you felt good, brother, don't stop to talk to me! You would swear you were doing something if you felt good and after talking to me, you wouldn't! Good old negative Norm! If you can't be a good sport, then screw it, right? Today I see people like me everywhere! I don't know if I had an influence on them or not! Today, positive thinking and positive living are the only way for me!

CLOUDY

Trying is good! Doing is better!

Even if every day doesn't seem to be full of sunshine, was it ever when you were using? Get honest now!

Daily Reminder
December 17

Think about it!

Even though I knew I was serious when I asked God for help on June 6, 1971, I didn't realize how serious I was until a number of years had passed and I was still clean! Like most addicts, many times in my using life, I pretended I was serious, but I was trying to scam Him—again! People told me many times, "When you get serious, so does He!" The only reason I got serious was because I didn't want to die! That was good enough for Him! Amen!

SERIOUS

Trying is good! Doing is better!

You can be too big for God to help, but you can't be too small! I'm living proof of that in both cases!

Norm Sharkey

Daily Reminder
December 18

Think about it!

Our reasons for getting clean really don't matter! We do have to have some good reasons if we want to stay clean! If you were scamming when you got clean and you continue to scam, I would be willing to say you will eventually go back to using and scamming! When we are stoned, we can play the game! When we are clean, our consciences won't allow us to play the game while everyone around us is being honest! We can't get our car up the mountain without gas; honesty is the fuel!

GET REAL!

Trying is good! Doing is better!

I think I can, I think I can! I thought I could, I thought I could! We knew you could, we knew we could!

Daily Reminder
December 19

Think about it!

That phrase, "The Great Spirit will only give us what we can handle," is a fact, both in problems and in answers! We can give in to drugs for either excuse! We can say, "I just couldn't take any more problems" or "I had so much success, I thought I would be able to handle drugs again." But folks, we were never able to handle drugs. Why do we think we can handle them again? Addiction is very, very sneaky! If we aren't aware, it will bite us up the ass every time, with no apologies!

GET REAL!

Trying is good! Doing is better!

Our best defense is honesty! Can I honestly say that I can handle drugs and not hurt anyone including myself? For me—no!

Norm Sharkey

**Daily Reminder
December 20**

Think about it!

Our lives, as far as we can remember, have been filled with fear and confusion. We tried to show people we had it together. When we were stoned, we had guts. Drugs gave us a false image of being solid.

GET REAL!

When we weren't stoned, the fear and confusion returned. Using to live and living to use does not make us solid people. Am I tired of being a fake? How can I change myself?

Trying is good! Doing is better!

*Drugs promise a lot but deliver nothing solid to stand on.
I must trust the people who are real if I want help.
Do I want help?*

Daily Reminder
December 21

Think about it!

Most of my life I have been in a cul-de-sac I created with drugs. Drugs told me that the way out of the dead end was better and stronger drugs. The more I used, the more I got lost. Drugs give us false messages and false feelings. **LIES** Drugs tell us not to trust a clean person, whether they are family or friends. How many stoned people can I trust with my life? Do they have it together, or are they also in a cul-de-sac?

Trying is good! Doing is better!

Have drugs made my life better or worse? If you answer your life is better, then don't waste your time with us. Go and use drugs! If you answer your life is worse, then ask for help! It is here!

Daily Reminder
December 22

Think about it!

GOD OR ME?

When we heard the word God, we thought it was a sick joke. If there is a God, why did He allow my life to become such a mess? If He loved me as much as some said He did, why did He keep me in the dead end? Was it God's fault, my family's fault, or my fault? Drugs would not let me see God's hope or my family's hope. Drugs are the friends of people with no hope! Drugs take us away from family, friends, and God.

Trying is good! Doing is better!

Is my life a mess because of God or because of drugs? How much longer will I trust drugs to make my life better? Is it possible that God can do what drugs cannot? Is it discussion time?

Sanity 365

**Daily Reminder
December 23**

Think about it!

Perhaps our family, friends, or other people have done us wrong in the past. How long must they pay for this? Usually when someone screwed us, we got even or tried to. Have we ever looked at the many, many, many times we've screwed someone else and felt no guilt? We felt it was okay if we did it, but it was not okay if it was done to us. Payback is a bitch! Afterward, we felt as empty as we did when we came down. So, like doing drugs, we did it again. Am I tired of feeling empty?

PAYBACK

Trying is good! Doing is better!

"I'm sorry" is hard for us to say and mean. If we are to stay clean, we must make a start. Who is the first person I will say, "I'm sorry" to?

Norm Sharkey

Daily Reminder
December 24

Think about it!

Guilt! This word kept me stoned for years. I got high trying to forget and ended up making more guilt. I felt guilty even when I had done nothing to feel that way because I knew the way I was living was useless

CHANGE

and selfish. The only help I ever gave anyone was to get him or her stoned so I could use him or her for something then or later. I was not able to give or receive love. I was lost!

Happy birthday, Andrew!
Trying is good! Doing is better!

Getting clean is the start! Getting clean with people will keep us clean in our guts, where we live, instead of in our heads while stoned! Start today with the person you have hurt the most—you!

Daily Reminder
December 25

Think about it!

On Christmas Day, the world was given a new light. Our new light was given when we decided to stop using. At first the light seems very dim, but each day it gets brighter as we do what we have to do. Sometimes we compare our light with the light of others who have been clean longer, and it looks very dim, but we must remember that they, too, started with a dim, small light. Ask them what they did to make their light so bright, and then try to follow.

THE LIGHT!

Happy birthday, Jesus!
Trying is good! Doing is better!

You are not expected to be perfect, just clean and better!

Norm Sharkey

**Daily Reminder
December 26**

Think about it!

WHO'S REAL?

Alone! Lonely! Lost! Even when we were with people, we felt that way. We were lost in a crowd! Drugs allowed us to feel connected, to feel normal, and to be part of what was happening. Little by little, we split from our real friends and convinced ourselves that our using friends were real people. More and more as we lost ourselves in drugs, our families and friends were pushed further and further away. There is a long road home, but we can get there.

Trying is good! Doing is better!

We may be on the right track, but if we just sit there, we'll get run over! Call or visit someone who can help you or who you can help. Even with a small light, you can brighten someone's day.

Daily Reminder
December 27

Think about it!

HOPE!

We may only be clean a few days or even hours, but even now we can see a future of hope. We can see that faint look of hope in the eyes of our family members and real friends when they look at us. They want to believe that we are serious about staying clean and willing to change. Am I going to tear their guts out by going back to what I was?

Trying is good! Doing is better!

Even if you are only one hour or one day clean, you can still help another addict. Just telling others what you have seen or heard from other addicts who are making it can be enough to help get them started. Do I know someone who needs help?

Norm Sharkey

Daily Reminder
December 28

Think about it!

Trusting people was something we stopped doing a long time ago. People always let us down! Instead, we put our trust in our dealers and in drugs. If our dealers said the drugs were good, we seldom questioned them and bought some. Even when we were ripped off, we still trusted our dealers. Why did we trust drugs again and again but not the people who really mattered in our lives?

UNDERSTAND?

Trying is good! Doing is better!

Have I or will I come to understand that drugs will deliver only jail, insanity, or death? When will I trust in something real before it's too late?

Daily Reminder
December 29

Think about it!

How do I become part of a group? If you are sick of the way you are living and want to get clean and change your life, you are in. It's that easy. There are no papers to fill out and no test to pass. "I want help. I need help," is all you have to say. You may think there is some hidden cost, but there is none. You have paid the price for years in the drugs you bought and the people's lives you sacrificed, including your own. Join our website at Sanity365.com.

JOIN US!

Trying is good! Doing is better!

I have decided today to begin a new life! I need help, and I want help! Please help me!

Norm Sharkey

**Daily Reminder
December 30**

Think about it!

You hear God or Jesus mentioned in recovery! Don't let this scare you or turn you off. When people say, "God, Jesus, or Higher Power," they are simply saying they have come to realize they don't have the power on their own to resist drugs and the old life. If you see a light in the eyes of someone from your group, it's God you see. Am I still afraid of God?

NO FEAR!

Trying is good! Doing is better!

Just saying, "God, Jesus, or Higher Power, please help me," is all you need to do to get started, and then fasten your seatbelt!

Daily Reminder
December 31

Think about it!

Many of us tried to get clean on our own. Sometimes we lasted a few weeks, a few days or a few minutes. Even when we had success, we weren't happy or content. If we are not happy getting clean, we will try again to get happy getting stoned. We must give this new life a fair shot. How long did we give drugs? Give up on drugs, not life! Clean is real; stoned is plastic.

SURRENDER!

Trying is good! Doing is better!

At the beginning of our drug use, life seemed like an endless trip of excitement! The odd bad trip is part of the deal! Then there are more bad trips than good ones! Finally, they are all bad! If you are still alive, you get clean!

CPSIA information can be obtained at www.ICGtesting.com
Printed in the USA
LVOW120017030212

266799LV00002B/7/P